FROM COMMAND TO EMPATHY

Praise for *From Command to Empathy*

'The world of work is rapidly changing because of technology and globalization, but it is impossible to predict where jobs will be. The only preparation for this new world is a strong foundation of basic skills, layered with an emotional intelligence, that makes us mindful, empathetic and resilient. This book does a wonderful job of thinking about emotions in the Indian workplace. With its rich brew of personal experiences and learnings, engaging case studies, research and questionnaires, *From Command to Empathy* is essential reading for employees and their leaders.'
—Manish Sabharwal, board member, Reserve Bank of India, and CEO, TeamLease

'As the world hurries towards a path of unsustainable growth and increased disparities, next generation of corporate leaders and managers will have to bring in empathy as an important element in running inclusive businesses. I sincerely believe this book will provide a direction to the younger generation of future CEOs, CTOs and CFOs—that pure business as usual will not work and they will have to bring in an environment or culture that combines heart and the mind.'
—Harish Hande, chairman, SELCO India, Ramon Magsaysay Award–winner and chosen by *Business Today* as one of the 'twenty-one young leaders for India's twenty-first century'

'Rapid changes in technology are disrupting the old order like never before. Professionals today need to constantly reinvent themselves to cope with these changes. Ironically, it is emotional maturity that will be required more than anything else to succeed in a world run by robots and machines. *From Command to Empathy* provides a well-researched and easy-to-apply framework of how to succeed in such an environment. An essential book for our times!'
—Hitesh Oberoi, co-promoter, MD and CEO, Naukri

'This book is one of the best books I have read on bringing EQ into the workplace. I loved the examples, case studies, assessment tools and excellent practical approach of the book. I highly recommend it to every Indian manager!'
—Prasad Kaipa, CEO Coach, board member, Indian School of Business, author of *From Smart to Wise* and TEDx speaker

'As nations progress economically, the nature of work moves from routine to being knowledge-intensive and creative. This necessitates leadership and management systems to evolve from being command and control–oriented to one that is based on trust, empathy, empowerment and inspiration. And key to that new style of leadership, according to the authors, is emotional enablement. This book is an important contribution that makes us sensitive to this evolving context and provides us with insights about how to get the best from people and organizations in this volatile, uncertain, complex and ambiguous world.'
—Sourav Mukherji, dean and professor of organizational behaviour, IIM–Bangalore

'I believe that EQ starts with self-awareness and if we are aware that we need to make a change in our lives, this book can be of great help. The authors bring together both cognition and emotion in a framework to transform the self. It is a must-read for all managers and leaders. More, if each one even practises a fraction of what is being read, [one] will see a sea change in one's work life and personal life for sure.'
—S.V. Nathan, chief talent officer, Deloitte India

'Today it is imperative for leaders to focus on empathy and inclusion in the workplace. This will help integrate the greater number of millennials and women professionals into the culture. In the history of Indian businesses, such an imperative takes us into unchartered territory. This is where *From Command to Empathy* makes its most

important contribution. Hard to put down—I cannot recommend this book enough!'
—Shradha Sharma, founder and CEO at YourStory Media, Fortune 40 under 40 and *ET*'s Promising Entrepreneurs of India Award–winner

'In today's era of competitiveness, being technically skilled just isn't enough. Building an empathetic culture is critical to building successful businesses. *From Command to Empathy* is one book that shows how emotional leadership can be the most important factor in driving your business goals. A must-read for all present and future leaders.'
—Dhimant Parekh, founder and CEO, TheBetterIndia.com

'I recommend [*From Command to Empathy*] to all leaders, technocrats and practitioners who believe that EQ will play an even more critical role in the future as we co-exist with machines that have equal or better IQ than humans. *From Command to Empathy* is a book that addresses this urgent need head-on.'
—Sachin Lulla, global vice president, IBM, rated top influencer for #IoT #Artificial Intelligence and #Watson

'Beyond just the reading pleasure, this book is an effective reference applied to the challenges the knowledge workforce of today is facing and struggling to deal with. The case study–driven style, combined with the ESTEEM framework, makes it real for the reader and provides creative insight to be both productive and popular in the workplace. *Command to Empathy* is critically relevant for the knowledge workforce of this century.'
—Tanmay Bandopadhyay, senior director, Johnson & Johnson LLC

'In today's VUCA (Volatile, Uncertain, Complex, Ambiguous) world, the one question everybody is struggling with is what are the skill sets required to do the jobs of the future. The book wonderfully combines the insightful business experiences of the authors with contemporary science and academics to provide a very simple framework for succeeding in business life by mastering your EQ. It is a very practical guide which can be used by millennials and others alike to not only succeed but find great satisfaction and joy in their work.'

—Vishal Bhola, global vice president, Unilever, Shanghai, China

'In the globalized business world of today, technology and tools tend to take the entire human dimension out of the equation! All the more reason why being realistic about goals, reflective of experiences and empathetic towards others at the workplace should form a critical aspect of our lives. *From Command to Empathy* totally nails this key imperative of the Digital Age.'

—Anoop Nambiar, chief data officer, HSBC Insurance

'This isn't the first book written on EQ—and won't, almost certainly, be the last—but it's the first that I've come across that has such a heavy Indian perspective while being global in its outlook. The reader will enjoy the many interesting and pertinent anecdotes that intersperse this scholarly yet engaging piece of work, as he also undoubtedly will the conversational tone of the narrative. Having had the good fortune of knowing Suman over a period of time and being a part of the admiring audience at a number of his "talks", I can vouch for the sincerity with which he and his co-author have approached this topic. I wish all principals, teachers and parents would read this book; there's much here—from Zen masters to mindfulness to millennials—that I am sure they'd relate to and benefit from. If we seek to build a society based on, borrowing an acronym from the book, ESTEEM and if tomorrow's society needs to be reflected in today's classroom, we'll certainly gain from the authors' perspective.'

—Santanu Das, president, Karnataka ICSE Schools Association, and principal, Sarala Birla Academy

'Today's fast-paced and result-oriented work culture comes with its pitfalls: the lack of understanding and empathy of senior management towards its employees. *From Command to Empathy* is the first book to address this highly relevant and critical issue, the missing emotional quotient in most Indian companies. This book is an eye-opener on a much-needed workplace reform, perhaps even an impending revolution in the making.'
—G.D. Gautama, former home secretary, Government of West Bengal

'Nowadays, start-ups are the new big thing. Entrepreneurs need to build relationships with and trust a whole host of people—employees, investors and clients. To navigate the many challenges on a daily basis, a high level of EQ will be the deciding factor between success and failure. *From Command to Empathy* provides a practical guide to steer through these complexities and make the right decisions. A great handbook for all current and aspiring entrepreneurs!'
—Ashu Garg, venture capitalist, general partner, Foundation Capital, San Francisco, USA

'Most skilled jobs will be automated in the future. What sets you apart is the Human Factor, your emotional quotient, your expertise in how you relate to other humans. This book teaches you exactly that—and more. Welcome to the future!'
—Avelo Roy, CEO, Kolkata Ventures, and TEDx speaker

'A well-written book with real-life examples that hit the message home. Many organizations and managers fail to appreciate the emotional intelligence needed to nurture and motivate their employees. Productivity and retention of employees is directly related to the emotional culture and the book captures it well. A must-read for new managers and companies trying to turn around their culture.'
—Raj Manchanda, PhD, chief development officer, Frequency Therapeutics, Boston, USA

'In today's changing job market, junior candidates are often at a loss as they embark on their careers. To be successful on a long-term basis, young professionals need to have a good degree of self-awareness, be realistic in their expectations and develop the ability to learn continuously through reflection. *From Command to Empathy* addresses all these aspects beautifully, and shows how to make it work. A must-read for all millennials!'
—Deepak Rathi, executive director and COO, HeadCount, an ABC Consultants initiative

'EQ lies at the heart of successful executive coaching. Although the concept is much in vogue, in reality, even seasoned leaders exhibit blind spots—being impatient, trying to prove oneself right, and not treating juniors with enough warmth. Recalibration thus becomes critical—pausing to connect back with oneself, at an emotional and psychological level. *From Command to Empathy* helps to do just that. A super-interesting book, with a framework, personal experiences, stories and case studies, that will engage, inform and inspire—a must book for every leader on the path to #BeTheStar.'
—Vikram Kalloo, executive coach, founding fellow, Harvard University Institute of Coaching, and TEDx speaker

'Contrary to widespread belief, achievements such as the Egyptian pyramids were not created by slaves but by free men inhabited by their will. In an economic world where religious beliefs are no longer such an effective engine, there are many theories that suggest models of leadership, to produce such prodigious results. In the book *From Command to Empathy*, Avik Chanda and Suman Ghose combine years of research and experience to offer a new grammar, based on the concept of empathy. What distinguishes this book from most others in the genre is its novelistic style of narration, interspersed with case studies, analyses and recipes for success, which make for an engaging reading experience and also benefit the reader in practical terms.'
—Gerald Gaillard, author of *The Routledge Dictionary of Anthropologists*

FROM COMMAND TO EMPATHY

Using EQ in the Age of Disruption

AVIK CHANDA AND SUMAN GHOSE

HARPER BUSINESS

First published in India by Harper Business
An imprint of HarperCollins *Publishers* 2017
4th Floor, Tower A, Building No. 10, DLF Cyber City,
DLF Phase II, Gurugram, Haryana – 122002
www.harpercollins.co.in

This edition published in paperback in India by Harper Business
An imprint of HarperCollins *Publishers* 2024

2 4 6 8 10 9 7 5 3

Copyright © Avik Chanda and Suman Ghose 2017, 2024

P-ISBN: 978-93-6213-146-1
E-ISBN: 978-93-5277-450-0

The views and opinions expressed in this book
are the authors' own and the facts are as reported by them,
and the publishers are not in any way liable for the same.

Avik Chanda and Suman Ghose assert the moral right
to be identified as the authors of this work.

All rights reserved. No part of this publication may be reproduced,
stored in a retrieval system, or transmitted, in any form or by any means,
electronic, mechanical, photocopying, recording or otherwise,
without the prior permission of the publishers.

Typeset in 11/13.8 Adobe Caslon Pro at
Manipal Digital Systems, Manipal

Printed and bound at
Manipal Technologies Limited

This book is printed on FSC® certified paper
which ensures responsible forest management.

Contents

Foreword by *Deb Deep Sengupta*	xiii
Preface	1
1. The Rise and Fall of Vineet: A Corporate Saga	11
2. Mission EQ: A Call for Action	29
3. Emotional Enablement: It's about Time!	48
4. How Do You Manage the Millennials?	74
5. From STEM to ESTEEM	93
6. Being Mindful: Alive and in the Moment	112
7. Being Realistic: Compassion, Motivation and Purpose	136
8. Being Reflective: Are You Missing the Big Picture?	157
9. Being Empathetic: Game, Set and Match	177
Index	202
References	205
Acknowledgements	215

Foreword

Deb Deep Sengupta

It's a myth that consumers buy products. What consumers buy is experience. Any organization that is in the business of providing products and services will fail if they do not first build the capacity to understand or feel what their customers and employees are experiencing from their frame of reference. This empathy in turn creates trust. Empathy cannot be built from just working behind a desk, or by reading about it. It comes from 'living' the problem, observing and understanding the challenge in real conditions. I strongly believe that there is enormous strength and innovative advantage that leaders can bring about in their organizations by adopting the empathy principle and instilling the same in their teams.

After all, teamwork and collaboration are the cornerstones of truly innovative organizations, as opposed to flashes of individual brilliance. The best leaders are those who have mastered the ability to strike a balance between recognizing individual talents and honing the potential of a collaborating team. And being self-aware and empathetic is at the core of what keeps a team going. By developing the ability to imagine oneself in the other's position, to understand what makes them tick and what motivates them, one can draw out more from a team than a sum of their individual capabilities. This empathy comes from using our reasoning abilities to understand the other person's thoughts and motives, and from truly making an effort to pause and reflect on the other person's perspective.

As a leader, one must be the example of 'working towards a higher purpose', since teams are better engaged and innovative when they know that what they do matters to others. And culture emerges from purposeful teams. For a leader, the ability to shape that kind of purposeful environment determines the legacy that they could leave behind.

In this context, *From Command to Empathy* is a timely book. The authors present the challenges and offer solutions, not theoretically but through the lens of practitioners who live this reality. The book takes the reader through multiple states of being: Being Mindful, Being Realistic, Being Reflective and Being Empathetic. This journey of self-transformation makes the book a practical guide that should be a companion for leaders as well as their team members.

Deb Deep Sengupta *is the president and MD of SAP India. In the* Harvard Business Review *study of the world's most empathetic companies, which we have referenced in our book, SAP stands in the top 10—the only technology company in the world to do so. SAP also stands at the vanguard of bringing about transformation through technological innovation, and is a model of what enterprises in a creative economy should aspire to be. In the corporate/services sector that is so much the focus of current discourse, this foreword makes the book all the more pertinent to all practitioners and enthusiasts interested in technology and innovation.*

Preface

Emotional Intelligence. Now.

'In the long run, EQ (emotional quotient) trumps IQ (Intelligence Quotient). Without being a source of energy for others, very little can be accomplished.' These are the words of Satya Nadella, CEO of Microsoft, addressing students at a Talent India summit.

Regrettably though, such a notion runs counter to the way we usually think. Even today, many leaders and employers focus on the need for greater efficiency, operational improvements and smarter management techniques to achieve bottom-line-driven results, at the expense of the human element involved. And the repercussions on the workforce are telling: an increased sense of alienation, greater stress levels, disillusionment and demotivation, all leading to lower productivity and higher attrition rates. The adverse effects are brought to light in even sharper relief when it comes to managing millennials, who are less hesitant than older generations of the workforce to leave a firm if its policies and attitudes don't align with their own values.

Studies show that empathy—which is about understanding others' feelings and emotions and our own impact on them—is more important to a successful business today than ever before, correlating to growth, productivity and earnings per employee. Here's a snapshot:

1. A study titled 'The relation between emotional intelligence and job performance: A meta-analysis' published in the *Journal of Organizational Behaviour* at Virginia Commonwealth University concludes that EQ is the strongest predictor of job performance.[1]
2. An analysis of more than 300 top-level executives from fifteen global companies showed that six emotional competencies distinguished the stars from the average.[2]
3. Research by the Centre for Creative Leadership has found that the primary cause of executive derailment involves deficits in emotional competence.
4. According to a 2013 study by American Express, EQ is one of the biggest predictors of performance in the workplace and a strong driver of leadership and personal excellence.

To objectively study the impact of empathy, a Global Empathy Index has been created, breaking down empathy into categories: ethics, leadership, company culture, brand perception, social media–driven messaging and ecological footprint. Using this Global Empathy Index, a *Harvard Business Review* study in 2016 found that the top 10 companies increased in value more than twice as much as the bottom 10, and generated 50 per cent more earnings. The correlation between departments with higher empathy and those with high performers was a staggering 80 per cent.

Now brace yourself for the real shocker.

The same study found that based on publicly available data, 6 of the 10 least empathetic companies in terms of the Global

---

1 E.H. O'Boyle, et al, 'The relation between emotional intelligence and job performance: A meta-analysis', *Journal of Organizational Behaviour*, Volume 32, Issue 5, July 2011, Virginia Commonwealth University
2 Cary Cherniss, 'The Business Case for Emotional Intelligence', *Consortium for Research on Emotional Intelligence in Organizations*, 1999, Rutgers University

Empathy Index are from India! And it's not as if low empathy values are limited to a particular industry or sector—these six giants spanned oil and gas, pharma, finance, telecom, technology and infrastructure.

This sort of evidence has been accumulating over the years and has now reached a level where it can no longer be ignored. Be it at the workplace or in our personal lives, the need to understand the concept of emotional enablement and to imbibe it in our lives is more important now than ever before.

And hence this book!

About the Book and about Us

What is the connection between empathy and leadership? How can emotional enablement help to meet both personal and business goals? Can an approach to management based on high emotional intelligence enhance performance of professionals? Is empathy at the workplace a one-way street, the onus being squarely on managers and business leaders—or do juniors share responsibility in this regard? Should training to build emotional enablement form a part of our educational curricula? And what measure of emotional maturity can be achieved relatively later in life, after one has already entered the workforce, or is even midway through one's career?

We try to answer these and other related questions in this book. We strongly feel that the concept of empathy is critical to the health of company culture and must take centre stage. At a time when employees clamber over each other to reach the top, the truth is that for business leaders to experience success, not only do they need to be sensitive to all the activity around them but also must they genuinely relate to the people they lead. It is imperative for the leaders of today to put themselves in their employees' shoes and view things through the latter's eyes.

In this book, we delve into the key problems faced by present-day professionals, and through various real-life examples drawn from industries across the world, we trace how the approach taken by leaders shapes the ethos of their organizations. We advocate the creation of an organizational culture that fosters trust as compared to command-and-control obedience, one which focuses on empowerment and not merely on authority.

Our research indicates that part of the unease with emotional enablement is a reflection of the way our education curricula are structured. We have simply not been trained for being self-aware or empathetic. For decades, world over, the focus has been on science, technology, engineering and mathematics—collectively referred to as STEM. This has been deemed to be essential for propelling rapid technology advances. However, this view typically diminishes the equally, if not more critical, human dimension. There is urgent need in the modern world for a more comprehensive, inclusive framework, one that augments STEM with this human component of paramount importance, to arrive at ESTEEM, where EE stands for 'emotional enablement'.

In order to develop the ESTEEM framework, we have gone beyond a pure educational schema, to explore the work of Daniel Goleman and other experts, whose research has paved the ground for the EQ discipline. We've leveraged our own experience, spoken with peers, studied the advances in neurosciences and organizational behaviour and ascertained the scientific underpinnings of our emotions, at the workplace and in our personal lives, to arrive at our conclusions. In our view, there are four major dimensions or 'States of Being'—Being Mindful, Being Realistic, Being Reflective and Being Empathetic—which help to move the needle along the EQ scale. Through discussions dedicated to each of these dimensions, we provide practical tips on how to get better at them and make them part of our daily lives.

We do not claim to be management gurus who have the last word on this subject. Or EQ gurus, for that matter. Our learning has been largely experiential and this, in turn, is what we've attempted to impart through this book. Between the two of us, we have over four decades of corporate experience, spanning business and technology consulting, programme management, business development and practice building. We have personally interacted with more than two thousand professionals, across age groups, seniority levels and a dozen countries.

Our tenure with consulting giants such as PricewaterhouseCoopers and Deloitte made us realize the power of empathy in breaking down barriers and opening doors in our relationship with clients and our own people. We've had the opportunity to interact with leaders in some of the world's most well-known organizations such as New York Life, Wells Fargo, Liberty Mutual, Adobe, Cadbury's, Philips, Intel, LG, as also government organizations in India and abroad.

We've worked with senior company directors and the junior-most interns at the workplace; we have observed how they operate in times of stress and crisis, their errors, and their triumphs in the face of adversity. Over the years, we've also evolved in our careers, gained insight and perspective, made our own share of mistakes and learnt from them. We've played organizational roles, built large teams, managed projects, provided training in leadership and consulting skills and mentored millennials.

And it is the sum total of this experience that we have distilled through this book. We hope that readers will benefit from the insights. We believe that the numerous personal anecdotes and real-life scenarios, questionnaires and self-scoring exercises presented throughout the book will make the reading experience more interactive and enriching.

How Our Book Is Structured

Chapters 1 and **2** recount a number of real-life experiences. In this introductory section, we highlight the need for emotional intelligence in the workplace. We explore the reasons why organizations typically shy away from discussing EQ. We show how EQ plays a key role in establishing a more empathetic culture in the organization. The old-school command-and-control style brings with it a certain mindset which is counterproductive in today's evolving organizations, in terms of both motivation and productivity.

What, then, defines an emotionally mature person—and how can these attributes be best demonstrated in the workplace? How is it different from expressing sympathy? Is it good enough to be simply 'listening' to problems, or is tangible, evident action required to demonstrate the genuineness of one's intentions? Why is empathy often misconstrued as a sign of weakness instead of strength, a tendency to 'give in' to demands of juniors, under pressure?

In **Chapter 3**, we explore the constituent elements of an emotionally enabled individual's personality and outline the different traits that the new-age professional requires. Case studies and instances from personal experience articulate how these attributes help in navigating today's environment and illustrate the typical challenges and roadblocks that you may face while embracing those traits.

Developing attributes such as listening skills, trust and sensitivity to cultural differences, self-awareness and detachment, especially in stressful situations, are all key to one's success as an emotionally intelligent leader. However, as this chapter shows, the important lesson here is not to exercise them in a purely transactional, silo-ed fashion—rather, to subsume them into an overall discipline of self-awareness.

In **Chapter 4**, we focus on millennials. A lot has been written about this generation. Misunderstood, vilified, defended or praised—no matter which side of the fence you are on, no one is quite indifferent to the millennials and the impact they create as the single largest cohort in the workplace. But what are the real aspirations of millennials as they enter the complex global workplace of today? Are they really all that different from the 'oldies' of the previous generation? Are they all about instant results and promotion or do they hold their own values and principles dearer than pay cheques and company shares? We examine these topics, using our own experience in working with and mentoring millennials, as well as studies specific to them.

In **Chapter 5**, we introduce a new framework: ESTEEM. The framework of STEM—which stands for the disciplines of science, technology, engineering and mathematics—has, for many decades now, formed the bedrock of the education system around the world. We show how an introduction of EE—emotional enablement—and, therefore, the transition from STEM to ESTEEM allow the seamless integration of emotional intelligence. We demonstrate why, especially in the context of globalization and India's growing involvement in the world economy, emotional enablement assumes an even greater role in shaping the destiny of organizations. Through real-life scenarios and viewpoints from experts and business leaders, we highlight specific nuances that warrant an even greater need for living the principles of EQ.

In **Chapter 6**, we focus on the first of the four states of being, namely mindfulness. It's about being in the moment, becoming more aware of what we're feeling, more thoughtful about our behaviours and more attentive to the impact we create on others. However, today, we are constantly running from one activity to the other; consequently, we are never in the moment, and we do not realize that this causes havoc in our lives. It prevents us from prioritizing our work, maintaining focus and keeping to deadlines. It also hampers our ability to connect emotionally with others. Ultimately, we lose touch with ourselves and end up leading shallow lives. We delve into the various factors causing this mindlessness such as bias for action and various distractions. We look at mindful meditation, among other techniques, and examine how we can use these techniques in our everyday lives.

Chapter 7 looks at the importance of being realistic. We all like to think that we are rational in our decision-making and in control of our lives at most times. But is that really true? Leaders often find themselves in situations where they take on unrealistic deadlines for their teams. While they may couch the challenge as 'stretch goals' to be achieved, their team views it as an impossibility, and falls prey to panic and low morale. And this happens because the decision-making in the first place has not been realistic.

Being realistic does not imply that we never aim high. We may indeed set our sights high, but at the same time, we need to find a mechanism of being able to reach these goals through several steps of continuous improvement and progress. We explore how, through a gradual, conscious process, we can infuse this quality of perseverance into our personality.

Chapter 8 is about being reflective, since in today's fast-paced world, we are often caught up in action mode with little time left for reflection. While action is critical to keep moving towards our goals and make us more efficient in our skills and jobs, reflection helps us in being more effective, i.e., by doing the right things, and not just doing things right. Being reflective helps in taking a very objective, dispassionate look at our actions and behaviours, associated emotions and feelings, and general state of mind. It is one of the best means of improving ourselves continuously, making course corrections and striving to achieve our goals.

Self-reflection can seem difficult at first, or even selfish or embarrassing. But like many other things, we will find that it becomes easier with practice and ultimately helps us become more effective and happier.

Chapter 9 focuses on the fourth state of being, namely being empathetic. Empathy is about both thinking and feeling. We need to use our reasoning ability to understand what the other person could be thinking, to feel how they must be feeling by putting ourselves in their shoes. But we need to be careful to avoid our natural tendency to overthink and start forming opinions. Unfortunately, although we have the intrinsic ability to feel for others, today's rushed lifestyle with increasing levels of negativity around us is making us hardened and dehumanized. The need of the hour is for us to start *feeling* once again. We need to be in tune with what that person or team is going through, so that we can respond in a manner that acknowledges their thoughts and feelings and thereby build and nurture trust, rather than destroy it.

How to Use This Book

Do you remember saying something hurtful to a loved one in the heat of an argument, only to regret it later? Or holding yourself back from being fully honest with a friend, fearing it would ruin your friendship? Have you fallen prey to road rage, told yourself that you wouldn't repeat the same mistake and then gone ahead and done it again? Have you felt tired instead of rejuvenated, after you are back from a break?

At work, have you wanted to speak to a colleague or senior about his rude or overly critical behaviour, but stopped yourself because you feel the other person might not take it well? Do you feel your equation with your team members leaves something to be desired? Do you wish you had a few colleagues, or even one person, whom you trusted implicitly and could reach out to without any apprehension during difficult times?

As a leader, do you believe you are quite approachable—and yet notice that your team members don't necessarily share that view? Have you ever got the feeling that you steered a meeting well, but found out later that the participants thought otherwise? Have you felt that your department's stretch target, instead of motivating your team, has instead had the opposite effect?

At a purely personal level, are you living true to yourself? Are you achieving your goals? Do you have clearly defined goals or are they more of a wish list? Do you struggle to respond when asked what your key strengths and weaknesses are?

If some of these scenarios resonate with you, this book is for you.

The journey of emotional enablement is a bit like learning a language that you are vaguely familiar with, but never had the time to apply yourself to. And as the saying goes—the best way to learn a language is to speak it. Therefore, while you become more knowledgeable about the four dimensions of emotional enablement, you would need to work on demonstrating it in your daily life and also be in a position to monitor progress for yourself.

Throughout this book, you will find questionnaires, tips and assessments that allow you to evaluate yourself along the different dimensions. Our recommendation is that you use them methodically—carve out time regularly to conduct an objective review and evaluation of yourself. At first, when you begin this process, you may feel that this is robbing you of yet one more hour or two, precious time that you don't have.

But we believe it will be well worth your effort.

1

The Rise and Fall of Vineet: A Corporate Saga

For many of us, 'twenty-four by seven' (24/7) has become a catchphrase that epitomizes our lives. It describes our personas as much as our lifestyles: perpetually on the go, intense work pressures, stiff competition, hectic travel schedules, and so on. It requires multitasking on personal and professional fronts, with no clear demarcation between the two. It also warrants high ability not just to adapt to it all but also to be eager and ready to take on new challenges as they come. One of the casualties in such a lifestyle (besides sleep!) is the dearth of time; consequently, there are fewer instances when one catches up with friends and does *not* talk about work. Each such meeting with friends therefore becomes something of an event, an occasion to be celebrated.

It was on one such happy occasion when, by chance, Avik and Suman were in the same town at the same time and decided to meet up after work at Toit, the popular pub in Bengaluru. The nice thing about pubs in this town is that you meet a lot of fellow professionals, but as the evening wears on, you end up exchanging stories instead of business cards.

It was a jam-packed Friday night and after waiting for a long time, drinks in hand, we finally got ourselves a table. Presently, a man came up, asking if we were expecting more company, and on being told that we weren't, squeezed in beside us with his drink. We were expecting him to be joined by someone, a colleague or friend, wife or significant other. Minutes passed, his first drink over, he went to the counter to order another and as he sat down again, it became apparent no one was claiming his company that bustling Friday night.

And yet company, it seemed, was what the man craved, as he frequently exchanged glances with us, then got drawn into our conversation and laughed out loud at a joke one of us had cracked. We introduced ourselves, talked shop for a few minutes, our new buddy insisting on buying us a round of drinks. And then, slowly, he started opening up. We'll call him Vineet. The story he shared will strike a chord with our readers.

Humble Beginnings

Vineet had much to be proud of. Humble beginnings: a small town in Punjab, where, through sheer grit and perseverance, he excelled in school, much to the surprise of elders in his joint family, who, being traditional small-time shop owners, had never set much store by education. Study further, beyond school? Whatever for? All that would fetch you was a degree and a lowly job in some office, pushing paper. Why not set up shop on your own instead, as your father and uncles have done? A well-run shop isn't likely to go out of business.

But Vineet persisted. He had to go to college, see the world, *do something* for himself. Eventually, a compromise was reached: They would send him to college, but he would have to earn his keep. While putting up at his uncle's in Delhi, he would need to lend a hand at the car repair workshop (of which his uncle was the co-proprietor) in the evenings, a condition Vineet gladly accepted.

The relocation to the capital was an eye-opener, in more ways than one. Delhi was an ocean unto itself. The sheer scale and enormity of things, monuments and forts, state buildings and offices, flyovers and main roads as massive as highways, people always moving, in a constant terrific state of hurry, to arrive, to achieve, to succeed. But amidst all this plenitude, Vineet noticed, there was a specific shortage: People were short on time and patience. Early on, Vineet realized he would need to take full charge of his own affairs, if he wanted to get ahead in a place like Delhi.

The Transformation

Strive, adapt and thrive—Vineet's formula for success. Over the next three years, a thirteen-hour day was normal, the commute to college, then the hours at the workshop, a hasty dinner, and finally burning the midnight oil with his books. But he gave his uncle no cause for complaint. Soon after his arrival in Delhi, he had realized how important communication was, to make an impression, a conviction he carried to this day and which had been instrumental in his success. And so, one of the first things Vineet did was to enrol himself in a spoken-English course.

Another round of drinks later, it was fast-forward to his new persona—Vineet the young corporate executive, his first job, that first pay cheque, the Maruti 800 bought on a bank loan, the first trip abroad. In terms of a facelift with people at home, the transformation was complete: Vineet, the bookworm renegade, had become a star. The lad spoke English like a sahib, wore snazzy suits, sat in an air-conditioned office and drove around the capital in a car bought with his own money. From the money Vineet saved up from his stints abroad, he paid the instalments for a new family shop in his hometown. His parents were ecstatic; what more could anyone wish for?

Breaking with tradition again, when it came to marriage, Vineet tied the knot with Simran, the girl he had met at a college fest. It was the first instance in his family of someone going for an alliance not arranged by the elders. But at home, things were now very different. He's no longer a kid, his Tau-ji had said; he has made his own way in the world, without anyone's backing, and this decision, too, will turn out to be opportune. The girl is from a well-to-do, respectable family. And, after all, he's not marrying outside the community.

It was a magical time that lasted for a long, wonderful stretch, Vineet recalled, a little emotion creeping into his voice, a time he felt would never come to an end. And the way he planned his career chart spoke of textbook-like precision and method: a sales job at first, then IT consulting, pursuing a correspondence master's course in business administration at the same time, segueing into a job in communication and training, his sweet spot, and finally, the present, much larger, people management role. His tenure in each job running no more than three years on average, never making a change without a level jump. And every time, a substantial pay hike.

He seemed to have a magical touch; all his plans had played out like clockwork. This current job, too, in the early days, was no exception. As if that too had been carefully planned, around this time, Vineet and his wife welcomed their first-born, Keerat. Career-wise, in shifting from sales to training and communications to this managerial role at a captive centre for an MNC, he had ventured outside his comfort zone. But now he stayed the course, remained with the company through its expansionary phase and reaped the benefits.

Increasingly, more work was being delivered from the offshore centre in Bengaluru. From an initial twenty-five members, Vineet's team size doubled in a span of four years, with a commensurate increase in his role, visibility and importance. A few months back, he had got his promotion, the second in four years that he had been with the company—Vineet was now associate vice president!

The First Signs of Trouble

Ironically, Vineet told us, it was at this point of his career that his troubles began. Earlier, when the team was much smaller, there was less responsibility in terms of deliverables. Moreover, earlier, Vineet had more say in the day-to-day running of his own team. The expansion of his team, Vineet realized, accompanied a corresponding downsizing of personnel located in the US. Times were hard and cost-cutting was felt to be an organization-wide imperative. Doing more with fewer, more cost-effective resources was critical.

This had many adverse effects. First, the US team came to see the expansion in jobs offshore as something that had happened directly at their expense. Every new offshore position meant a potential job lost in the US. But more significantly, as the offshore team came to be a more key part of running business operations for the organization, its workings also came under the microscope. Soon, Vineet was starting to feel that even with a fifty-member team, he was effectively operating like a team member, with multiple layers of management in the US to report to.

To add to his woes, since the various centres in the US were spread across different time zones, Vineet found his workday steadily expanding to well beyond twelve hours. In the morning, almost as soon as he woke up, he would feel compelled to check the emails that had come in overnight. Always—at least this was the impression he was given by higher-ups—his team was behind on something or the other, so that even the little time Vineet spent with his family became somewhat guilt-ridden. Similarly, after he got back home in the evening, there would be another call or two with the onsite team. And yet more mails, before he could finally call it a day.

None of this helped things at home. Earlier, Simran was working as well; but ever since their daughter Keerat was born, she had taken a break from work, and was now totally confined to the flat. On the other hand, thanks to his increased work pressure, Vineet was spending less time at home than before—and even when he was around, he was usually tired, stressed out, distracted or annoyed. Or on calls. Making him unavailable for his share of the household chores or even a relaxed dinner out.

As Keerat started to grow older, Simran said she would like to take up a job again and she would therefore need Vineet to 'pitch in' a lot more, dropping their daughter off to school sometimes or helping with her homework. Surely, this wasn't asking for much? But with his insane working hours, how was that going to be managed? She was happy that Vineet had got his promotion, but not at such a high price. And it was beginning to affect his health, his sleep cycles. More often than not, he brought home his work pressures and irritability, unable to relax even over the weekends ... this job had taken over his whole life; didn't he see that? Why not look out for a more suitable opening that gave him more time for his family, she wondered aloud, maybe go back to his old job?

Simran would complain about the lack of time they had together. Of course, since Keerat was still quite small, they couldn't think of partying or going out like they used to earlier, something that both of them had enjoyed. But couldn't Vineet at least take a few days off during Diwali, so that they could fly to Delhi and be with her family? And then a longer holiday over the Christmas–New Year time frame, when even offices in the US would be shut down? Could he at least do that much?

Vineet struggled to explain to her that the US being on holiday actually put a greater onus on the offshore team, to help carry on business and provide 24/7 coverage across the globe during the period. Bottom line: no long holidays for the family around Diwali or Christmas, although he was quick to suggest that she could always take Keerat to Delhi. That only made it worse. While, as a professional, Simran understood the logic of what Vineet was saying, as his wife, this further deepened her sense of feeling marginalized.

Arguments began to break out frequently between the two of them, something that had seldom occurred before. Recently, during one such spat, Vineet recounted, Simran had told him that if he couldn't spare any time for his family, she might as well relocate back to Delhi, where at least she had family backup and support. This knocked the sails right out of Vineet. Ever since their college days, he and Simran had been inseparable and the mere prospect of such a situation was devastating for him to contemplate. He tried to make some adjustments to his routine, got back home a bit earlier at times, took advantage of his company policy to work from home once a week. But even these measures, Vineet felt, weren't effective.

Things weren't going too well at work either. If Vineet was feeling stressed with his swelling workload, his team members didn't seem to fare any better. They complained that there was too much for them to handle. They had to get into calls, working very late hours and reporting back at the usual time the next morning; things were taking a toll on people's family lives, their health. They all felt as if they were working round the clock, with no respite or recognition. And Vineet sensed that this was a subtle message from the team that just as the onsite leads were not being appreciative of their efforts, neither was he.

Eager to turn things around, Vineet decided to spend more time with his team; meetings and calls became more frequent, with larger groups as well as individual team members, as did working lunches and even the odd weekend stint, when Vineet felt that the team needed to catch up on backlog. Through this approach, he reasoned, there would be a better bonding between him and the team and he would also be more hands-on, with a better grip of ground realities.

At first, Vineet thought this had a positive effect on overall motivation levels, but after a while, he realized that his team members were trying to avoid going into these meetings. They had enough on their plates and these 'deep-dive' sessions were construed as micromanagement and a burden on their already cluttered schedules. Also, these meetings were eating into Vineet's own time. So he began to phase them out. He had to admit this team-building strategy was a failure; this forced him to introspect on the problems again.

One of the main issues, he realized, was that even with fifty full-time personnel, the offshore team was spread quite thin. The very nature of work allocation across geographies required additional checks and balances, communication and reporting. Also, the offshore teams had not been ramped up to the extent that their onsite counterparts had scaled down. And this in turn led to a basic imbalance between resources and workload, resulting in the current situation.

To deal with the problem at its root, Vineet created a business case for ramping up the offshore team, taking inputs from his own juniors, and then sent it through to his onsite counterparts. He gave his team to understand (something Vineet regretted later) that he was taking up this issue with the senior management group onsite and should be able to do something about it. To his surprise and disappointment, his plan did not find favour with the leadership team at his company's HQ.

To makes matters worse, Sumit, his country manager with site responsibility for overall offshore operations, demanded to know why this plan had not been discussed with him first. Without proper deliberation and approvals, the plan shouldn't have gone to the onsite leaders in the first place! This caught Vineet off guard, since his functional reporting was to the US and he did not feel the need to align with Sumit on this.

This incident alerted Vineet to another acute problem—he sensed that there were underlying trust issues between onsite and offshore, resulting in low empowerment offshore.

Previously, Vineet told us, he shared a good rapport with the senior management team in India; in fact, the person who recruited him was an approachable, easy-going leader who believed in empowering his team, taking suggestions and hearing people out. However, this person had since moved on. And following his own promotion, Vineet had been engaging directly with the US and this had never been questioned. So, when Sumit questioned him on why he was not consulted, he saw this as a fallout of unclear delineation of roles and responsibilities.

Vineet was finding it increasingly difficult to work in this environment where he didn't feel empowered. About the problems with his own team, he had once tried to discuss it with his US bosses but they simply didn't have time for other people's worries. And he couldn't broach it again, for fear of sounding inefficient and weak. At home, Simran could also not be expected to spend the little time they had together listening to his office-related issues.

Things came to a head around Diwali. While the US folks were aware of the festival, their expectation was that the offshore work would continue uninterrupted. In reality, though, most team members in Bengaluru had requested for leave in advance. When the risk was brought to Vineet's notice, his initial reaction was to discuss the situation with the onsite team. But in the light of what had transpired recently with his proposed ramp-up plan, he decided to inform the country manager this time, lest he be ticked off again.

But Sumit, on hearing of the issue, just shook it off. *Ask the team members to adjust their holidays to the extent possible.* Those who had made travel plans should be requested to take their laptops along and work remotely during the period. It was made clear that these 'requests' in question were, in fact, mandates. And of course, it was Vineet who had to convey this to the team. This was his problem, his team. This created even more bad blood, with Vineet now feeling totally alienated from his team.

Particularly difficult to handle was the group of five campus hires who had joined his team earlier in the year. Fresh out of college, Vineet told us, 'these kids of today' came with an innate sense of entitlement, questioning everything—processes, protocol and even his own leadership. They demanded constant, individual attention and special treatment, not content to follow instructions unless they were first convinced of the approach. They demanded to be taken along, not led; what they wanted to do was to collaborate, not just obey. And when did Vineet have the time to coach, mentor and motivate them on an individual basis? He was struggling to keep up with his own workload.

Each of these new hires gave Vineet reasons why even working from home around Diwali wasn't a tenable option. No scope for negotiation or reaching a compromise. Things heated up with one of these new hires, and Vineet lost his cool, berating him in front of the team for his lack of professional ethics and commitment. This ugly spat was not without further adverse repercussions.

Shortly afterwards, that same team member who had been criticized publicly by Vineet put in his papers. During the exit interview, he cited Vineet's aggressive, micromanaging leadership style and uncaring attitude towards juniors as one of the main factors behind his decision. Subsequently, the HR team had a discussion with Vineet, playing back the issues communicated to them. And

Vineet grew concerned that soon the other campus hires in his team might follow suit, which would severely dent his standing as a leader, permanently damaging his reputation in the company.

Everything around him was deteriorating. And although Vineet could identify and isolate all these problems that kept surfacing, he couldn't come up with solutions to tackle them all. The cumulative effect was overwhelming. He had become more irritable at work, losing his temper, snapping easily at delays and defects. Occasionally, Vineet admitted, he would go for a few drinks on his own, after work, just to clear his head, think things through. When he got home, much as he hated it, he would tell Simran he was out at a team dinner. He felt guilty about it, but he just couldn't help it—he just had to get away from it all, at least sometimes!

The Heart of the Matter

It was quite late by now but none of us was hungry. Some finger food arrived, which we started to nibble indifferently. Vineet had gone quiet momentarily, shaking his head. It was clear that all these things he had told us had been bottled up inside him for quite some time, bursting to come out. We had touched a raw nerve and he had desperately needed to talk to us, draw us to the heart of his problems in search of a solution, an option which he didn't seem to have either at his workplace or at home. Inwardly, he was seething. His inability to cope with his situation had become intolerable. His every look was an invitation for us to ask him questions, challenge his actions, so that he could then give us his perspective. And so, careful not to appear intrusive, we did.

So, you're saying the issue over the Diwali holidays has made you the villain as far as your team is concerned?

Totally! I had assumed that the onsite guys knew about it already—and then that rude awakening. But it's not inflexibility on my part, you know, which is the real issue here. That's just the way things are in my office. Unfortunately, that's the work culture, and

I can't change it on my own. I had nothing against an extra couple of days off for the team. I need that too, right. But I told you what Sumit's reaction was. How could I override his decision? And who would manage expectations with the onsite team?

Maybe your team sees you in the same way as you view your bosses?

Hmm ... yeah, you're right to some extent. While I have the intent to do what is right for the team, often my hands are tied without any support from leadership both onsite and offshore. And then I become the guy who is always dishing out bad news to the team.

Perhaps you can still salvage the situation with the other campus hires who are still around, in your team?

I'd love to, but don't see how. It's not like taking them out for coffee or lunch would do it. They need focused attention, each one of them, and where do I have the time for it? At the same time, you can't spoon-feed them—then they feel insulted. And once an impression sets in, it's very difficult to dislodge. With these campus kids, to be honest, I have a hard time figuring out what makes them tick. They have a problem working late hours, a problem working weekends. And that guy, who complained against me when he quit—that just took the cake! The problem is that with these people, every task completed demands instant appreciation. I mean, we were once twenty-year-olds ourselves, right ... tell me, did we act like that at their age?

You don't agree with their point of view?

Well, I agree that they need a bit of autonomy and breathing space. But again, that's company culture, isn't it? A single person can't drive it. And when management is bureaucratic and into micromanagement, well, that's the attitude you're propagating down the line.

And your equation with the onsite folks also leaves something to be desired, correct?

Absolutely! I want that relationship to be more equal, for a start. Take the Diwali example. OK, granted that in this instance there was a bit of screw-up at our end, but I'll tell you something ... Even if we had informed them in advance, onsite would have still grumbled.

Just because there's a reporting relationship shouldn't mean we take people for granted. The US shuts down over the Christmas period, so why grudge us our holidays?

Then there's the home front. Perhaps it makes sense for you to take some leave, focus on things at home?

I've been planning to do that for a while now. Whatever transpires, I can't afford to have problems getting out of hand at home. Just waiting for things to ease out a little bit at work—but that's not likely. For most of the time that Simran and I have been together, you know, we've been a happy-go-lucky couple ... we'd go for drives, holidays, partying all the time ... even though our resources were far more limited. Today, we seem to have the money but ... Earlier, if there was any trouble at all at work, I'd come home and discuss it with her. Not anymore, though. These days, the little spare time that we do have is taken up talking about Keerat. The 'me time' is suddenly gone. I really feel like an oldie though I'm still in my thirties.

So, are you thinking of a change, like your wife suggested?

Yeah, I've started looking out. But you know what the market is like these days, not the easiest thing to land a job, especially once you reach a certain level of seniority. Anyway, let's see ... what worries me a lot is the financial insecurity of things. We've just moved into the new flat, there's a big EMI on it. And with Simran not working at the moment, if I were to ... mean, if I lose my job...

Closing time. And here was Vineet, still raring to go. But then, realizing embarrassedly that we had stayed behind just to listen to him, he thanked both of us profusely. As we were leaving the pub, we caught a last glimpse of Vineet, alone again with his thoughts. He looked completely gutted.

Have You Ever Felt Like Vineet?

Vineet found himself in a situation that seemed intractable. Even though, as a mature, intelligent senior professional, he could identify many of the areas of concern, he had no solutions for them. As work and stress piled up at the office and he became less popular among co-workers, he grew defensive and isolated.

You might say that Vineet's behaviour towards his co-workers, especially his juniors, was reactive and transactional, that he lacked the basic connect with his people, that he did not have empathy or at least was not able to demonstrate it. Over time, Vineet's increased irritability, impatience and criticism of his team members alienated him from them; rather than take initiative on their own, they adopted a reactive approach, doing only what was specifically instructed. The unpleasant incident with the new employee created a ripple effect, as the other team members became uneasy opening in his presence, particularly when their opinions were at variance with his. In fact, following that incident, the others began to be intimidated, bracing themselves for something similar to happen to them. What is striking is that the ground reality amidst all this was rather different from what Vineet himself perceived it to be. In his own view, he was a victim of circumstances.

What could Vineet have done differently, not to just avoid the unpleasant situations but to guide effectively his team during crises and emerge as a natural leader? While there's no formulaic answer, following are some of the questions he could have asked himself:

- Do I have a network of colleagues with whom I share a lot of trust, who not only feel comfortable approaching me but also will 'keep me honest'?
- Do I have a coach or mentor within the organization? If not, how can I identify such an individual and develop this relationship?
- Am I overcommitting, overselling to my team, clients or stakeholders, promising things I'll be struggling to deliver?
- How inclusive am I in my decision-making process or when it comes to handling crises? What can I do to have team members find me more approachable?
- How often do I demand privileges, directly or indirectly on account of my position in the company?
- Am I mature enough to own up to my mistakes?

A predicament such as the one Vineet found himself in is not rare. Increasingly, for all of us, there is the pressure to address personal and professional imperatives concurrently, amidst ever-diminishing margins of error. But when we hear someone else's story, the defence mechanism inside us kicks in. *That could never happen to me*—is the most natural reaction. Or, *I'd have reacted differently under the circumstances*.

But to what extent is that true? You are aware that your behaviour has an impact on those you're interacting with. Crises at the workplace warrant speedy decisions. You find yourself caught up in the heat of the moment and yet, no matter how high the pressures are, the expectation is for you to act swiftly and calmly, in a mature fashion, driving tensions and conflicts to amicable conclusions. This requires a deep understanding of your strengths and weaknesses, as well as control over your emotions. It also entails a good understanding of others' strengths, values, motivations and emotions, an ability to emotionally connect with others, build rapport with them and get things done. In short, there is a pressing need for emotional intelligence, or EQ.

Self-assessment

Now, as we come to the end of this chapter, put yourself in Vineet's position and take the exercise below. Remember that all the circumstances and constraints described in his account still hold. The only leeway is that of your response—and with that, the ability to change the outcome of events. Consider the following situations and circle the option that is the closest fit to your own response.

Situation #1

Your team members have been complaining that they are overworked.
Your response:

1. Even though you know that the team is stretched thin, you still tell them that they will need to manage the excess workload since extra resourcing is not possible.
2. Discuss with your boss about extra resourcing, after taking inputs from your team. You tell the team that they should expect to see changes on this front soon.
3. Conduct due diligence to confirm that the increased workload cannot be handled more efficiently within the current team. Equipped with a business case for the extra resourcing, you take up the matter with the relevant stakeholders. You communicate results to the team only if you are successful in achieving your goal.

Situation #2

There are concerns from senior management about the quality of work delivered by your team. Your team comprises a team lead and junior team members. Your own due diligence shows up instances where the team has indeed dropped the ball.
Your response:

1. Call a team meeting, tell everyone they're slacking, point out the lacunae in their work and lose your temper when they try to explain their point of view.
2. Call over the team lead for a 1:1 meeting around the quality-related issues and clearly communicate to him the leadership's displeasure. Ask for a detailed report in two days' time.
3. Meet with the team lead to understand the challenges faced by them and participate in conducting a root-cause-analysis of the current escalation. You then call a team meeting to reinforce your commitment to support and guide them.

Situation #3

Certain incidents in office lead you to believe that there is growing distance between you and the team that you manage. They are seeing you as being increasingly disconnected with their issues and concerns.

Your response:

1. Have a discussion with your boss—and the HR team, if necessary, to tell them that in spite of the help and guidance you're offering, there is an overall low level of performance in your team. Thus, they should not get surprised if they hear complaints from the team members.
2. You feel the reasons that the team is demotivated are not related to you but more to do with the organization culture. Hence there isn't much you can do about it. While you allow the team to voice their concerns, you just try to manage the 'noise'.
3. Invest considerable time and effort to understand what is causing the rift and build relationships. You encourage the team to speak their minds and you try to be more inclusive in your decision-making.

Situation #4

You and your team have been putting in a lot of hours at work over the past several months. This is expected to continue for some more time. A vacation opportunity presents itself around the Christmas holidays and your spouse is keen for you to take some time off from work, travel and spend quality time with the family.

Your response:

1. Take your holiday, delegating all your tasks among team members. You have been stretching for a long time at work and deserve a break.

2. Forgo your holidays. The team must be around during the holiday season and it'd look bad if you weren't around. Also, they would need your supervision.
3. Plan a roster of tasks and resources in advance, for the holiday period. Schedule your vacation but make others comfortable with the tasks delegated to them. Keep all stakeholders posted on the plan and be available on the phone, in case of very urgent issues.

Situation #5

Around 11 p.m. on a workday, you receive an escalation mail about a deliverable from your team seeking quick response and resolution.

Your response:

1. Take no action. The following morning, your team will automatically pick it up as they come in to work.
2. Make a note of the query, bring it up with the team next morning and ensure that it is addressed with the importance it deserves.
3. Check immediately on the urgency of the deliverable and whether it can wait till the next morning. If not, mobilize resources and solve the issue that same night. Follow it up with root-cause-analysis to prevent such a recurrence going forward.

Here's how to interpret your scores:

If your score is between **5** and **8** or below, you have a tendency to act defensively when faced with tricky situations. There are many real-life examples and case studies in this book that can help you in dealing with situations.

If your scores are between **9** and **12**, it indicates that you act with maturity and discernment and you could work on doing so more consistently. Through the course of this book, you will be able to identify the specific attributes that will need additional focus, to bring about greater consistency in emotionally mature actions.

If your scores are between **13** and **15**, then you already have a good understanding of how to handle difficult situations with tact, poise and emotional maturity. Continue to imbibe learnings from more such examples.

In case your score from this initial exercise is somewhat disappointing, don't be discouraged. Reaching an evolved and permanent state of emotional enablement is a journey. And given time, discipline and practice, it's totally within your reach to develop the skills required to do so. Once there, you will find that you are in a better position to deal with exigencies, being armed with methodical approach and tools with which to enhance your emotional maturity. And equipping you with these tools is what this book is all about.

2

Mission EQ: A Call for Action

In the middle of a hectic week at work, Swati, a high-performing programmer in a large MNC, goes up to her boss and requests immediate leave.

'I just got a call. My mother's been taken critically ill and admitted to hospital. There's nobody else at home to take care of things…'

The manager, Rajesh, who is amid an escalation in his project, looks up from his computer.

'What's that? How come you didn't tell me before?'

'I just got to know about it … right now!'

'How long do you suppose you'd be away?'

'That's the thing! I don't know any details, except that suddenly, she had to be hospitalized. I need to leave now please…'

Now Rajesh looks genuinely worried. 'Have you worked out a replacement?' he asks.

Swati is shattered. Under other circumstances, had she asked for unplanned leave without any such exigency looming on the horizon, Rajesh's reaction would have seemed natural, perhaps even justified. But in this instance, with Swati going through a personal crisis, the situation required careful and empathetic handling. Instead, what she got was an unthinking, knee-jerk reaction.

'What hurt most,' Swati recounted to us later, 'was this complete apathy in a person whom all this while I had looked up to as a mentor and supporter. I had really thought this was someone I could turn to in my hour of need. Rajesh was my direct supervisor in my earlier project as well, and we had always shared such a good rapport. That made his uncaring words all the more painful.'

And because of this insensitive behaviour on Rajesh's part, beneath the veneer of corporate savvy, irrevocable fault lines appeared in a professional relationship that had been going strong for years. Rajesh did allow Swati to go on leave but the way she had been made to feel preyed on her mind, and after she resumed work, the distance between them gradually grew and could not be reconciled.

What was more damaging was that Swati started equating Rajesh's behaviour with the general ethos of the management, and within a year, she left the organization. It was therefore a double blow, as the company lost a committed and talented employee, who, but for this incident, would have stayed on with the firm.

The Need for Emotional Intelligence

Incidents such as these, which need to be tackled with considerable emotional maturity, occur all around us and perhaps with more regularity than we'd like to admit. Not only is it worrying that such situations have ceased to disturb us, but also more alarmingly, there almost seems to be a tacit, subliminal acceptance that this is how things generally are. Increasingly, we come to see these experiences as a sort of constant in our lives, as things that we just need to grit our teeth and endure as best as we can; we assume we're powerless to change them. So, expectations from others are not just lowered; they undergo a fundamental shift, especially regarding leaders in the workplace. Being task-driven and result-oriented are seen as hallmarks of character in a strong leader; in fact, we expect such traits to be demonstrated, even if these come at the expense of compromising interpersonal relationships.

On the other hand, a genuinely empathetic leader is sometimes viewed as 'soft' and therefore not effective. Perhaps, hardened by the intense competition we face daily at the workplace, which instils in us a kind of 'zero-sum game' mentality, there is even a sense of mistrust when it comes to empathy. A tendency to treat with suspicion any notion of altruism, so that when someone does us a good turn at work, there's mistrust in accepting it at face value. Instead, we begin to ask ourselves—*Why is this person going out of his way to help me? What does he stand to gain by it?*

Have we as a society become so immured within the boundaries of traditional command-and-control thinking—which espouses the tenets of putting task above means and advocating a top-down, even autocratic, style of management—that we have relegated to the position of an afterthought the one element that stands at the heart of it all and without which things would come to a standstill, namely, the human dimension?

The answer is perhaps a conglomerate of lingering old-school ideas, hypotheses and myths, coupled with practical challenges. Which in turn leads to avoidance of any serious discussion about emotional intelligence and the fundamental role it plays in defining an organization's culture, the motivational level of its workforce, the level of productivity and eventually, the performance of the organization.

The role of emotional intelligence in the workplace (especially from the perspective of leadership) has been in vogue for around two decades now. Since the 1990s, Daniel Goleman, eminent psychologist and former science reporter for the *New York Times*, has been advocating the cause of emotional intelligence through a series of groundbreaking works.[1] In these highly researched books, based on advances in neuroscience and social psychology, Dr Goleman argues that as high a proportion as 90 per cent of top performers have much higher EQ than average; that, typically, an individual's role in any job comprised 58 per cent work that require EQ instead of IQ, increasing to 71 per cent for senior leadership, with only 29 per cent input based on technical skills at that level.

If we asked a random set of managers as to whether they would relate to Rajesh were they placed in the same situation, and whether his behaviour would resemble their own, we might hear quite a different story. This is primarily because most of us believe that we are pretty high on emotional maturity. After all, how many people typically identify raising their emotional maturity as an area of improvement in their annual goals or development plans? And therein lies the problem—those who most need to develop it are the ones who least realize it.[2]

In Rajesh's instance, when senior leadership later gave him feedback that he needed to have handled the situation differently, at first, he was completely taken aback, convinced that they had it wrong. When pressed further, Rajesh became totally defensive, saying that it was the crisis, the stress of the project he was going through at that moment, which made him react like that, and that under normal circumstances, he would never have done so. Rather than face up to the reality of the situation, he chose to dissociate himself from it. 'That's just not me!' he protested. The fact remains that Rajesh simply didn't have the requisite self-awareness or empathy that is a key hallmark of emotional intelligence.

While Rajesh may not have realized it himself, when his colleagues and subordinates were asked to describe him, they would say things like—'He's a bull in a china shop'... 'He's a task master'... 'He is good to you only as long as you are of use to him'. The truth is, these kinds of traits are often pretty obvious to the people around the person exhibiting them but not to that person himself!

Say, you are entrusted with a very important assignment with a tight deadline. For starters, you hold others to the same high expectations you set for yourself. You have a clear, well thought-out plan for how to make the project successful. You discuss the plan with your team and defend the plan with rigour. As days go by and the deadline approaches, you increase the level of communication in team meetings. However, you often feel like others don't get the point and it makes you impatient and frustrated. Your attempts to alleviate the situation and lighten the mood in team meetings backfire and you think your teammates are being oversensitive.

Sounds familiar, right? If so, you may be in for a surprise. As we shall see in subsequent chapters, the responses above are clear signs that you need to work on your emotional intelligence!

There is one factor that plays a key role in determining how we act in any given situation—context. Simply put, our behaviour is a function of the environment, but also of the mood and criticality of the moment. Even those of us who are ordinarily sensitive to matters requiring emotional intelligence may end up acting quite differently under pressure or in crisis situations. This holds true for most people working in any organization. As Rajesh himself admitted, had he not been undergoing an escalation in his project at the point when Swati spoke to him, he would probably have handled the situation better.

But then, do circumstances give one an excuse to be less empathetic and absolve oneself by blaming external conditions? Unfortunately, we judge ourselves by intent and judge others by their behaviour. Swati's judgement of Rajesh was based on how Rajesh behaved at that moment irrespective of what his intent was or how much pressure he was under. Often, we don't realize the powerful impact our words and gestures can have on those we interact with. A single incident demonstrating low empathy can create a rupture between people—the kind we saw in Swati's case—from which we may not fully recover. Therefore, it becomes imperative that we strive to maintain our emotional equilibrium at all times, irrespective of the situation we may find ourselves in.

While this is hard to do, it is something that can be learned, practised and, to a large extent, mastered, even beyond the formative years in life. Goleman shows that contrary to what some people believe, attributes of emotional intelligence (especially inner strength in the face of adversity) can be learnt and inculcated. Great bosses are known to be calm in times of crisis; in fact, it is their ability to not let the situation get the better of them that makes them great in their people's eyes.[3]

So Why Is EQ Important?

With a growing proportion of repetitive skills getting automated, what remains are the more complex, non-repetitive jobs, which tend to be multidimensional in nature. Today, it's not just about recalling information or executing an idea according to a predefined project plan, but about analysing situations, weighing options, evaluating decisions and generating new ideas and ways of viewing things.

Imagine you're fresh out of college, working as a programmer in the IT sector. While specific programming languages are primary skills you're expected to possess, they're by no means the only ones. Being part of a global delivery team, the ability to communicate, collaborate and influence becomes essential to the entire delivery process. And if project teams are located across geographies, this places additional expectations on you, including the ability to work with people with different accents and cultures, and an evolved sensitization to varied cultural nuances.

Couple of years down the line, you may be put in charge of a small team comprising, say, three to five juniors. The skill set you are expected to have now expands substantially. Besides pure technical knowledge, several other aspects, such as the onus of people management, delivery management, risk mitigation, issue resolution and reporting now come into focus—a complex matrix of skills that need to be learned and constantly calibrated, in the light of experience. As our job roles become more complex, there is greater need for a highly evolved style of human interaction and emotional maturity.

If your project manager asks you—'*Are you on schedule with your unit testing?*'—that's relatively easy to answer, provided you're on track and are knowledgeable about your domain skills. On the other hand, if the question is—'*Do you have everything you need to effect the change in your code?*'—this touches on various aspects of organizational culture, change management, conflict resolution, collaboration and communication. And a response can trigger another set of questions, equally complex in nature, such as the ones below:

- Who has requested the change in the code? Has the change-control process been followed, reviewed and signed off?
- Who are your stakeholders for the design pertaining to this code? Have you discussed and aligned your approach with them?
- What is the quantum and impact of this change on other parts of the design?

A Call for Action—Suman's Story

Equipped with emotional intelligence, Rajesh would have responded in a more appropriate manner, thereby keeping the situation from spiralling out of control. But EQ goes much deeper than being able to say the right things at the right time. It is about leadership and character—words need to be followed up with action because relationships are built around authenticity and trust.

Sometimes things get clouded when, whether unconsciously or by design, the responses we meet with are associated not with action, but rather the mimicry of it. This happens when we encounter people who, while appearing to be concerned, do not go beyond the preliminary stage where one's viewpoint is heard, one's concerns are encouraged to be articulated and some corrective course of action is hinted at as well. But it is precisely because those initial reactions seem so genuine that it takes time for us to realize their ultimate ineffectiveness.

Here is one such story.

> This was back in 1997. I had just got my degree from IIM-B, married my fiancée and landed an enviable job in a leading global manufacturing company. It was a global managers programme and I was among a select few to be based out of Seoul under direct appointment of the Chairman's office. Everything was perfect!

But with the passing of a week or two following our arrival, the charm of my new surroundings wore off and certain challenges that I had not anticipated began to present themselves: an alien cuisine; absence of the heightened level of interaction one sees in India all the time, even in the workplace; and colleagues frequently slipping into Korean during meetings and discussions. This last bit, the non-inclusiveness of the culture at work, was disconcerting and I decided to speak to my boss about it. He gave me a patient hearing, never interrupting, and at the end of it, nodded seriously and said—'I'm concerned.' I waited for him to say more, and he did—'This should be addressed.'

I was impressed. Here was someone who did not react defensively and was mature enough to internalize all my concerns; he would surely do something about it. A week went by, then another, but nothing on the ground changed. I relayed this conversation with my manager to a colleague, an American on deputation for the same programme and who, like me, had faced similar challenges. He merely shrugged and said, 'Don't hope much. I've had a similar experience with him. He makes all the friendly noises, but nothing beyond that.'

And then something happened that exacerbated the issues I had been facing till that point. It was a Friday afternoon and I had planned to take my wife out for dinner. Around the time we usually left work, we were all called in by a supervisor to attend a working session. This was important and could we all attend please? Refreshments and food would be served. The meeting lasted till 8 a.m. the following morning, which is when I finally got to leave office. Back at the hotel, I found my wife frantic and weeping. This was before the era of WhatsApp and instant messaging, and because nobody else had left the room through the night (incredible as that may sound!), I had somehow found it very difficult to excuse myself, get to a landline and call my wife.

> But things had now come to a head. I scheduled a meeting with my boss and shared my concerns more vocally. Work was important, but on this occasion, it had disrupted things badly on the personal front. What if this repeated? Going forward, we should at least have a process whereby attendees are given adequate notice. When I finished voicing my angst at length, my boss, putting on an utterly serious expression, said: 'Yes, I hear you. We need to fix this.'
>
> It was only then that I realized that my manager's immediate reaction to any such issue was in each case also his final one. It was merely his way of diffusing an immediate concern, with no backed-up intention of actually doing something about it.

As we learn from this account, it is obvious that emotional intelligence (EQ) goes way beyond 'listening' skills and customary responses and involves the inculcation of a particular mindset. In this case, Suman's manager was found wanting not just in action, but in a larger mix of several highly subtle qualities, including reflectiveness and openness to change.

The world today is characterized by globalization, increased automation and the proliferation of rapidly evolving and often disruptive technology. However, most leaders and employers take this change in a restrictive sense, implying the need for greater efficiency, operational improvements and smarter management techniques focused on achieving hard, bottom-line–driven metrics. This approach, while necessary to keep pace with advances in process and technology, usually overlooks the human element and the key role that it plays in motivating people, energizing teams and channelling them to secure favourable outcomes and success for the organization.

The repercussions on talent and workforce are telling: an increased sense of alienation in the workplace, greater stress levels, disillusionment and demotivation, leading to lower productivity and higher turnover rates. The effects are brought to light in even sharper relief when it comes to managing millennials, because millennials not only demand to know the organization's purpose—its reason for being—but also are less hesitant (than older generations of the workforce) to leave the firm if that purpose doesn't align with their own values.

Researchers argue that contrary to the belief of emotional intelligence being an intangible quality without a direct correlation to performance in the workplace, it did actually have an adverse effect on organizations where this was not manifested in the culture.[4] Leaders with qualities that entail a high level of emotional intelligence have often gone on to distinguish themselves in the workplace. Likewise, leaders high on IQ but lacking in EQ often find it difficult to steer through choppy waters.

Consider the case of Rahul Yadav. An IIT-dropout, he founded Housing.com while still in his early twenties and took it to fantastic heights within a remarkably short time frame, making his company one of the most sought-after start-ups, and himself the flamboyant Young Turk the whole nation followed and looked up to.

However, this meteoric rise was followed by a less savoury period, as during his tenure as CEO, Rahul found himself getting mired in one controversy after another. From taking potshots at other industry leaders—making derogatory comments about them, disregarding the advice of the investors and his board—to the notoriously controversial responses during his 'Ask Me Anything' sessions, his image swiftly changed from the quintessential whizkid to the enfant terrible of the industry.

Yadav's attitude began to have adverse impact on market perception and confidence in his leadership. Things came to such a crisis point that, eventually, the board of Housing.com was forced to fire its own founder and CEO. According to the board of the company, 'Rahul Yadav's behaviour towards investors, partners and the media was not befitting of a CEO and was detrimental to the company'.

In Rahul Yadav's case, while his natural business savvy was exceptional and attributes such as 'drive to achieve' were very pronounced, they directly clashed with other qualities, such as empathy, impulse control and reflectiveness. His overt aggressiveness at the expense of attributes that are critical to successful interaction with peers, colleagues, investors, analysts and critics exposed his lack of empathy and sensitivity when dealing with people as well as situations, leading to his ouster from the very company he founded.

Getting a Second Chance

They say life rarely gives us a second chance. A situation occurs, we react on the fly, the moment passes, and only much later do we realize the import of what we might have said. How often is it the case that you regret something said in the heat of the moment? You're too proud to apologize to the person whom you may have hurt, but somehow absolve yourself, saying: 'It's all in the past; I can't do anything about it now. But lesson learnt. Going forward, I won't react like that.' Yet, when a similar situation presents itself again, how prepared are you, in the light of previous experience, to deal with it and, consequently, how different is your behaviour from the earlier instance?

Suppose our manager Rajesh too got a real second chance and in the light of hindsight, could shape his responses. The interaction could now go something like this:

'Rajesh, I just got a call—my mother's been taken critically ill and admitted to hospital. There's nobody else at home to take care of things…'

'Oh … yes, of course you should go. Do you have means of transport?'

'No. I usually take the shuttle to work.'

'Hang on then, let me call the travel desk; they'll be able to get you a cab in a few minutes.'

'Thanks, that'd be helpful! Rajesh ... there's quite a lot of work on my plate today.'

'Don't worry, I'll have someone in the team pick it up for now. Just give me a quick list of your tasks while you wait for the cab.'

'I have the list on my desk...'

'Great! We'll take it on from there. Swati, I know this must be a very difficult time but let me say this—if there's anything you need, anything at all, give us a buzz, okay? We're all here and more than happy to help.'

Now imagine yourself in Swati's position. How different is this interaction with your supervisor from what we saw in the beginning of this chapter?

Building Relationships through Positive Emotions

Emotional intelligence, or its absence, bears vital import not just at the workplace. All of us exhibit telltale signs of EQ in our everyday lives, in our regular interactions with people around us. What we say—sometimes, even what we don't say—can have a significant impact on people we interact with. A kind word or a disapproving frown at a critical moment can subtly change the nature of your relationship with another person. The more mindful you are of this power of communication and expression, the more sensitive you are likely to be to situations as they evolve, and the more emotionally mature your responses are likely to be.[5] We all know the oft-quoted adage—*Think before you react*—but how difficult is it to actually follow it in real life? And how can we gauge the effectiveness of our own responses?

We have by now seen several instances where emotional intelligence plays a vital role in keeping emotions and behaviours in check, even in high pressure and crisis situations. But interestingly, an emotional connection gets formed not only during situations of adversity but also through ones that involve positive emotions.

The way we respond when others share good news with us directly builds or undermines those relationships. Research findings based on studying fulfilled couples indicate that supporting one's partner when good things happen is equally, if not more, important for the health of the relationship than supporting them when bad things happen.

One approach to learning how to build relationships by focusing on good news is through a technique called Active Constructive Responding (ACR). Proposed by psychologists Gable, Reis, Impett and Asher,[6] this is a widely used framework for analysing responses to situations and grading them in terms of emotional effectiveness.

A consistent, diligent practice of this approach can help you to be more aware of your responses to situations, build empathy and sensitivity and, consequently, develop the ability to build lasting relationships. Our responses could be either constructive or destructive (what we say) and either active or passive (how we say it). Of the four possible combinations, the only one that builds emotional connection is the type of response that falls in the Active Constructive zone.

Apply this framework to yourself by considering the following scenario:

You meet up for lunch with a friend who tells you with visible excitement: 'Guess what—I got my promotion.'

Now consider four potential, distinctly different responses given below.

A: 'Oh, good for you.' But you say nothing further, perhaps because you're preoccupied with something else. Since it is such a brief response, there is little or no active emotional expression from your side. While your response is not negative, you don't share your friend's joy and enthusiasm. And your response is also a conversation killer.

B: 'Let me tell you about my appraisal discussion.' You are impervious to your friend's obvious happiness and sense of accomplishment. There is probably little or no eye contact; instead of hearing and sharing his joy, you hijack the conversation and quickly turn it around to make it about yourself!

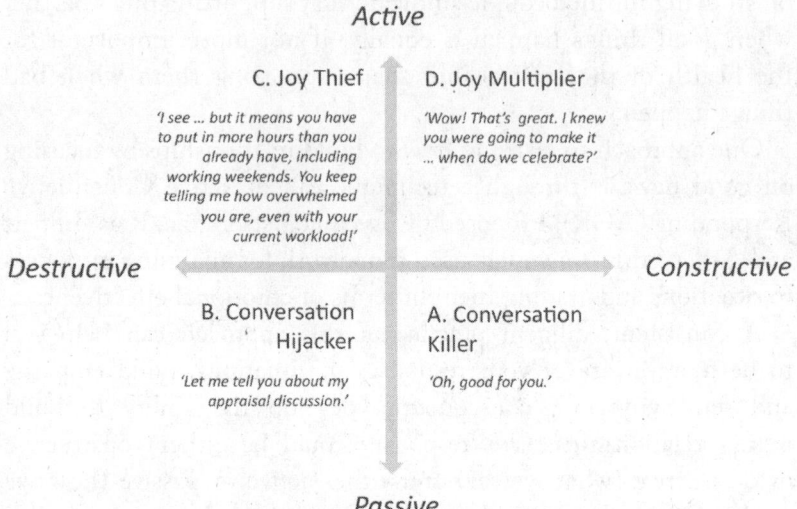

Figure 2.1: An illustration of ACR Response Mapping

C: 'I see ... but it means you have to put in more hours than you already have, including working weekends. You keep telling me how overwhelmed you are, even with your current workload!' Your body language (such as your frowning) conveys negative emotions and your deeply pessimistic response steals his joy, not only negating your friend's accomplishment but also calling into question whether it was worth it.

D: 'Wow! That is great. I knew you were going to make it ... when do we celebrate?' You are genuinely pleased and excited at your friend's success, and your body language, of maintaining eye contact and displaying positive emotions through genuine smiling, touching, etc., clearly shows the other person that you are happy for him. Of the four types of response, this is the only one that connects emotionally and positively and reinforces the human connection.

All these four responses may seem equally spontaneous and, depending on your mood at that moment, plausible. We often respond in all of the four ways depending on various factors such as our state of mind at that moment, who it is we are interacting with, our past interaction with that person, and how frequently we interact with that person.

So, while a conversation once a fortnight with a sibling who is based in another part of the world will typically be quite empathetic, our responses to an immediate family member could be different given the frequency of those interactions. Think of the different ways you respond to your child when he spends more time engrossed in sports or music instead of studying and you will immediately understand the power of the ACR matrix!

The clear majority of social interactions is 'real-time', allowing very little leeway for processing information. Therefore, thoughtful contemplation is key to ensuring we respond with emotional intelligence. Typically, if we are reacting to a situation, responses #A, B, C, or variations thereof are likely outcomes. Only with practice of thoughtful contemplation will response #D start emerging as the natural response.

Measure Your Own EQ

As we have seen, self-awareness—in other words, being conscious of how emotionally enabled you are is a good place to start.

Apply yourself to the following test. Each of the scenarios below outlines a typical situation at the workplace, along with a predefined response. Use the score card to grade yourself against each scenario and in the blank space, enter the score that most accurately describes you, in that situation.

It is important for you to score against every question. If your feel that any of the scenarios are not applicable to you—for those queries, imagine yourself to be in the situation described and score yourself accordingly.

1 = the response stated never applies to you
2 = the response stated rarely applies to you
3 = the response stated sometimes applies to you
4 = the response stated often applies to you
5 = the response stated always applies to you

Scenario #1

Situation	Your Response	Score
You have scheduled an important meeting, and a team member who was to provide the key updates does not show up at the scheduled time. He then walks in casually into the meeting fifteen minutes later, and you lose your cool.	It gets you angry but just before you lash out, you realize that you have lost your temper and do not make that evident in front of the team.	

Scenario #2

Situation	Your Response	Score
It has been a stressful week: long hours, tough meetings, missed deadlines and an unpleasant evaluation feedback that you have had to give to a direct report. When you get home late, your spouse asks you to help your son with his maths homework.	You do not let your office pressure influence either your decision to start with the homework or your mood while teaching your son.	

Scenario #3

Situation	Your Response	Score
Staying back late in office for a client call, you have taken flak for the quality of a deliverable that a colleague of yours is responsible for. The colleague has left office early that day. This makes you angry with him.	Next morning, when your colleague comes in to work—you greet him as usual before having a chat with him on the previous day's incident.	

Scenario #4		
Situation	Your Response	Score
A team member comes to you asking for advice on an issue; yet once you begin to do so, she starts to challenge what you are saying, putting up reasons why they would not work.	Realizing that she is not being receptive, you do not argue with her. Instead, you ask her to take time to think over your suggestions and then schedule another meeting later with you.	

Scenario #5		
Situation	Your Response	Score
At a family dinner over the weekend, you receive a call from an irate supervisor, berating you over the quality of a report you had handed in several days ago; he wants to know how you plan to rectify the situation.	You assure him you will have the plan worked out by first thing Monday morning and return to the dinner table without letting this situation upset the home front.	

Scenario #6		
Situation	Your Response	Score
Late afternoon on a working day, your boss comes over to your desk and requests that you take on some pending tasks from a colleague who has had to go on unplanned leave, due to a personal situation. He is aware you have quite a bit on your plate already, but would like you to help out.	You tell your boss that you have your plate full and hence would need some reprioritization to be able to take on the new load; you do not let the new load impact you emotionally.	

Scenario #7

Situation	Your Response	Score
A conversation with a colleague turns emotional as he starts telling you about his mother who is undergoing treatment for cancer—and how this is affecting his life.	Recognizing his need to speak to someone about this, you cancel your coffee break and give him an empathetic hearing.	

Scenario #8

Situation	Your Response	Score
Lately, your boss seems distanced from you, whether in response to a greeting or during team meetings.	Instead of trying to second-guess the possible reasons for his behaviour, you schedule a meeting with him to clear the air.	

Scenario #9

Situation	Your Response	Score
At a 1:1 meeting, you have given some hard feedback to a direct report. Thereafter, you notice that he is avoiding you.	You realize that your words may have hurt him and it calls for another discussion, preferably an informal one to get things back on track.	

Scenario #10

Situation	Your Response	Score
A new joinee who has been onboarded to your team comes up and introduces herself. She asks if you have some time during the day for a catch-up. You have a very busy day ahead of you.	You give her a few minutes of your time to hear what she has to say, instead of delegating the conversation to a subordinate.	

If your scores are between **10** and **23**, then emotional enablement is not yet an area of strength for you. Read through the examples and case studies in the book, try to apply the principles of EQ to your daily life and take the assessment again after a period of time, say six months.

If your scores are between **24** and **37**, it indicates that you have the workings of emotional intelligence embedded in your personality. As you work through this book, try to identify the specific attributes that need more work and sharpen your skills around those.

If your scores are between **38** and **50**, then you already have a mature measure of emotional enablement. Continue to imbibe the learnings from this book and practise them in your daily life.

3

Emotional Enablement: It's about Time!

The World in Transition

What makes emotional intelligence so important today, at an organizational level? If getting the job done is all that matters, why invest so much time and energy in building and sustaining relationships with co-workers? And why does it hurt if a few of these so-called 'relationships' get strained or broken along the way? After all, people with any given set of skills are replaceable and some element of 'churn' in the workplace may actually be healthy. If traditional economic theory is anything to go by, labour is just another resource, a factor of production to be used, like land and capital. So how important is the human element really? A large part of the answer can be attributed to the age we live in, and the constantly evolving demands thereof. Human civilization and expectations have seen a paradigm shift, especially when contrasted with the days of the Industrial Revolution.

At the advent of the Industrial Revolution, from an environment of manually crafted garments and tools, there was a swift, abrupt transition to an era of mechanization and assembly line–based production across a whole range of products. Mass production became the order of the day. Such a model required repetition and consistency; for example, a worker filling boxes with the production line output had to do the same tasks over and over again through his long shift. Jobs and skills were narrowly defined, based on the division of labour. Roles were created within organizations by replicating these jobs on a large scale.

A key success factor in making this model work was to instil a sense of stringent discipline among all workers across stages of production. The worker filling boxes was supposed to do his job repeatedly without mistakes, and also do it increasingly faster, to improve productivity. This necessitated a command-and-control style of management, with the supervisor handing out instructions for battalions of factory workers to carry out to the letter.

As time passed and technology saw vast advancement, these jobs got considerably more complicated. The process of manufacturing a steam engine was inherently more complicated than that of making a shoe. Many more processes and steps were involved, generating new roles and jobs. And while each of these roles required unique skills, they were still quite narrowly defined. As production increased, manufacturers grew by enjoying economies of scale and were able to sell their products universally, without effecting much change in the product mix.

The diagram below presents a snapshot of the changes brought about by technology and automation, and the impact made by them at both individual and organizational levels.

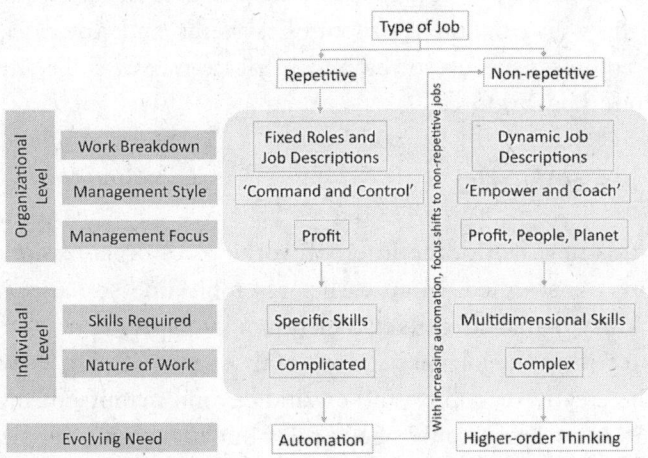

Figure 3.1: Impact of repetitive and non-repetitive jobs

Today, with the wide adoption of newer technologies, automation, gadgetry and the Internet of Things in everyday life, there is need for a more complex and sophisticated blend of skills and behaviours. While an increasing number of routine, repetitive jobs are being automated, the ones that remain and the new positions that are created require higher-order thinking and creativity to fully exploit the power of technology and continually fine-tune processes to align with the technology and the environment.

This explains why, along with increasing technology, paradoxically, the search for human talent is at an all-time high. While there is a larger workforce at the disposal of organizations today, employers are complaining more and more about not finding the 'right people'. Organizations need to be able to attract, train and retain their good people as they are not easily replaceable. And this is what makes the process of nurturing relationships in the workplace so important.

Let us return to the search for the 'right people'. Why is there this gap between what organizations demand and what they typically find in the market? That is because, on the one hand, there's the expectation for a more evolved, multifaceted mindset, but on the other, relatively few people are able to make the transition in their competencies, attitudes and work ethic, to match this need. At the same time, organizations are also trying to keep pace with the rapid progress in technology, changes in consumer behaviour, tastes and preferences, by changing their structures, systems and processes. This again requires a more evolved and intricate mix of skills and attributes from the workforce.

A Brave New World

To cater to this new world, the internal workings of organizations are also being transformed. In an earlier assembly-line scenario, it was about clearly demarcated roles which required specific tasks to be carried out within the job descriptions of those roles. Today, as we move into the creative economy and expand beyond manufacturing to services, it is no longer only about roles but also about people.

It's about finding the right people and carving out roles for them. Earlier, within the roles, certain set actions had to be carried out specific to the roles. But increasingly, it is not just action but also interaction between people.

The transition from 'responsibility' to 'ownership' is another case in point. Responsibility is something that is *given* to a person whereas ownership is *taken*. As jobs get complex with more touch points with people, the lines of responsibility blur, and in such a situation, it requires a sense of ownership to ensure that the process runs successfully across the value chain. While giving responsibility is required, what is essential is ownership.

In a traditional set-up, the organization is held together with a clear structure and hard-line reporting. In the evolving scenario, while the 'hard' organizational structure continues to exist within an enterprise, it is the 'loosely coupled' network of people or connection between people that is driving interaction, both internally and with the market.

As the shift happens from a command-and-control style of management to a more inclusive, bottom-up approach, energy and mindset—more than power—are what are moving companies forward. Hence, energy replaces power as the fuel driving the organization. Influence plays a much more important role than authority in getting things done in this new organization. People form deeper bonds with community which goes beyond individual departments.

The focus shifts from production in the earlier paradigm to synergy and collaboration between people for continually creating new products and services as also co-creating, which often means moving outside the walls of the enterprise by collaborating with the ecosystem. The factors that drive people also undergo transformation—shifting from external drivers such as financial incentives to something that comes more from within such as internal motivation and passion. Wisdom, rather than just knowledge, is the need of the hour—the ability to create original work and/or draw connections among ideas rather than just being able to remember, recall and repeat facts and concepts.

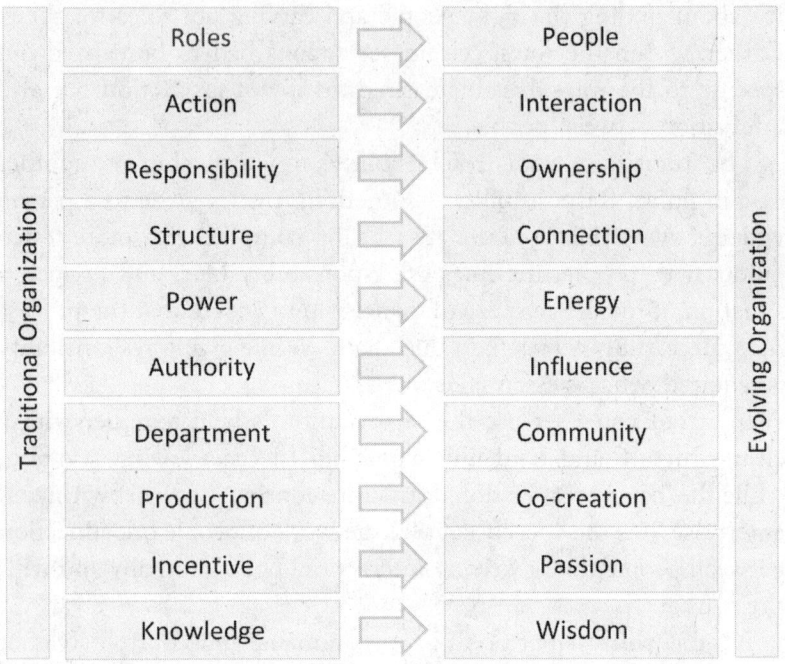

Figure 3.2: The nature of the evolving organization

As Figure 3.2 shows, in the evolving organization, the human dimension assumes a much more prominent place than it did in the traditional organization. Traits and concepts such as ownership, connection, energy, influence, community and passion are really all about people.

Consequently, management sciences such as statistics, data analysis, productivity and financial controls are things we can almost take for granted these days. They are still necessary but not sufficient to make the transition to a great organization. There is an urgent need to master the management arts over and above the management sciences. The arts comprise the human dimension—qualities that define leadership, integrity and character—things like vision, passion, persuasion, commitment, listening and ethics are all key to building great organizations.

The Need for Organizations to Change

In the past, organizations had but one paramount goal—the maximization of profit and shareholder value. But in our present era, a company's performance is guided just as much by the image it projects to its customers and the world at large. Besides production and sales targets, additional expectations—emotional, social and ecological—are now placed on them. The key enablers making this shift possible have been social media and technology. Today, news travels almost real time across the world. If an oil spill happens anywhere or a major corporate is sued for fraudulent practices, we come to know of it almost instantaneously, wherever we are.

How an organization treats people—whether employees, suppliers or customers—plays an important role in the way it is perceived. Does it have an employee-friendly culture? What inclusive measures does it take to ensure greater participation of women? What is the company's track record in employing people from less privileged backgrounds? What measures does it take to make its operations environment-friendly? If the company's values do not align with a customer's own values, that in itself can end up hurting the company. In short, expectations from organizations around the world today are centred on this principle: that they be economically, ethically and socially sustainable.[1]

Take the case of Apple, which faced criticism for not helping the FBI to write code that would help unlock a phone that's part of a terrorist investigation. Advanced encryption techniques have made digital communication impervious to surveillance, thereby threatening security because it sets up safe communication channels for terrorists. Apple's main argument for not cooperating was losing the trust of customers by collaborating in an enterprise that compromises individual privacy. But for customers who feel that helping to fight terrorism is more important, this may cause a dent in the image and perception of Apple.

Being Human in the Digital Age

Organizations are not trusted if they are not honest with themselves. Therefore, there is constant pressure on leaders to be proactive, transparent and inclusive with their employees. First and foremost, they need to act with integrity and their decisions need to be ethical. With empowerment comes accountability. A single incident can swiftly snowball into a crisis, if the communication around it is not managed well. The British Petroleum (BP) oil spill of 2010 is a case in point.

In what was one of the worst oil spills in recent history, an explosion killed eleven workers and injured several others in an oil rig, in the Gulf of Mexico. BP's immediate response was to try and deflect blame onto the owner of the oil rig and order its own employees not to talk to the media. But there was a huge backlash from the public, mostly as a reaction to media reports, and this put a dent in BP's trustworthy public image. Ultimately, BP had to change its stance and take full responsibility for the spill.

Today, more and more companies are proactively engaging with the public instead of trying to keep them at bay. Take Shell, for example, which runs a programme called TellShell, where a customer can log in complaints and get a response from the company. By taking corrective action and learning from its mistakes, the company can continue to improve its service levels. And this is what the India site looks like:

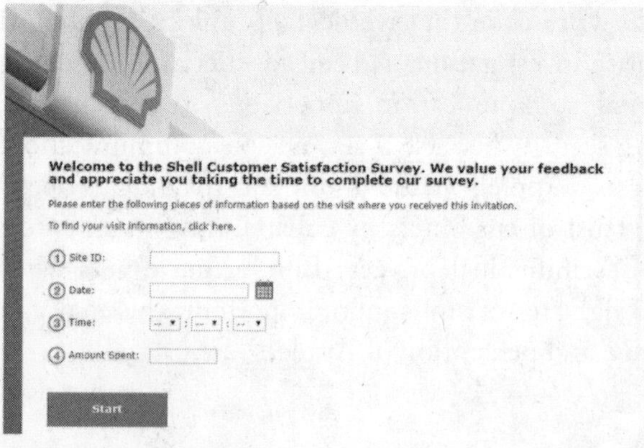

Figure 3.3: TellShell India homepage

Despite full intention of being proactive, there are events that leave customers disappointed. On 6 October 2014, Flipkart ran a huge sales event, where more than 1.5 million people shopped on their website, clocking a record $100 million worth of sales in just 10 hours. The company was, however, not prepared for the sheer scale of the event. There were outages on the website and issues relating to price changes, out-of-stock issues and cancellations. But the owners, Sachin and Binny Bansal issued an open letter to all its customers. In it, they conveyed their unconditional apology, explained what led to some of those issues and what actions the company was taking to ensure such a mishap would not repeat.

As is evident from such instances, it is critical that the collecting, processing and conveying of information to stakeholders is done in a careful and appropriate manner. The need to be emotionally engaged with employees and customers is felt more strongly than ever before. Research shows that effective employee engagement is one of the chief imperatives of leaders across the globe. Engagement is seen as not just effective communication and involvement but also a genuine investment by the leadership team in getting to know their people better, empowering them and including them in the decision-making process.

Such investment has a direct and positive impact on the loyalty and motivation level of employees, and immediate supervisors have a huge role to play. Workforce engagement is higher when team leads (a) have some form of daily communication with their team members, (b) empower them to feel comfortable in talking about any subject and (c) personally help them develop in their roles. The demonstrated ability of being personally engaged with one's team members plays a key role in its overall functioning and success.[2]

That said, we continue to see instances where leaders begin with well-meaning objectives but lack the determination to see them through. After some initial, tenuous steps, their plans start to falter, something else at work takes priority, and people go back to their old ways of knee-jerk reactions and didactic leadership. This affects morale and productivity down the line. At an individual level, it engenders a lack of clarity around decision-making, the feeling of being overwhelmed by work and of being distanced from others.

And that's when things start to veer out of control. Jim Loehr and Tony Schwartz, in their book *The Power of Full Engagement*, describe the situation aptly:

> When demand exceeds our capacity, we begin to make expedient choices that get us through our days and nights, but take a toll over time ... Faced with relentless demands at work, we become short-tempered and easily distracted. We return home from long days at work feeling exhausted and often experience our families not as a source of joy and renewal, but as one more demand in an already overburdened life.[3]

Ask yourself how many times you felt like this over the past year. At some point or the other in our working lives, most of us have. So, are the challenges that leaders face truly external and beyond their control? Can leaders act in ways to affect a different outcome? And what about factors that stem from the personality, anxieties, fears or insecurities of leaders?

The Power Paradox

One of the main considerations is the way the attainment of authority and power affects one's behaviour towards others. Psychologists have a term for this: the power paradox. Studies show that a person may at one point exhibit all the qualities and attributes suitable for a position of leadership, power and trust. Yet, on attaining a position of power, over time, those very qualities get eroded.[4]

Portrayals of such figures abound in popular culture—literature, plays and films are full of examples. One can recall Emiliano Zapata, the famous Mexican revolutionary, immortalized by Marlon Brando in the eponymous movie, *Viva Zapata!* Towards the beginning of the movie, the would-be leader, who is still an ordinary peasant, goes to meet a brutal landowner to protest an injustice. But that man has no patience for such a petition; when Zapata persists, the landowner glares at him and asks, 'What's your name?' There's an all-too palpable threat underscoring his question.

Almost two decades later, Zapata the revolutionary is now a law unto himself; the seduction of power is complete. A petitioner comes to Zapata with a grievance. Zapata attempts to brush him off but the man will have his say. Enraged, Zapata barks at him: 'What's your name?' The irony here is stirring and undeniable.

If we look around in our immediate environment, we may find instances of individuals who at one time were easy to work with, cared about their team members, and had the ability to motivate them and lead from the front. But as their careers progressed and new responsibilities took them to ever greater heights of power, they appear to have shed those very traits and qualities that made them stand out as natural, popular leaders in the first place.

Then, the inevitable happens. Such a person walks into a meeting and the conversation that was in progress comes to an abrupt halt, the energy level in the room dips. No one wants to contradict the leader, who, through subtle and sometimes overt means, is telling the group that he is always right. Juniors and even peers are uncomfortable about voicing their opinions and concerns, let alone disagreements. And so, over time, the leader becomes isolated in his ivory tower, losing the ability to connect with his people.

But why does such a phenomenon take place with almost metronomic regularity, across industries, cultures and geographies? And why is it so often associated with instances when people are promoted to the ranks of management? Research conducted on this topic shows that accession to power can actually interfere with our ability to empathize with people in situations removed from our own.[5] Empirical studies by Dacher Keltner, author and social psychologist at the University of California, Berkeley, demonstrate that people who have power are shown to suffer deficits in empathy, the ability to read emotions, as well as the flexibility to adapt their behaviour to match other people's behaviour.

A variant of this scenario is one in which people, despite themselves, elect individuals who they know are likely to be insensitive and self-serving to positions of power. Part of the reason for this is the fact that often the traits that get people to power—visibly exuded confidence, drive, determination and a certain charismatic brashness—aren't necessarily the ones best suited to keep them there. But it could also be that people tend to confuse confidence for competence.[6]

For people who are leaderless or have had a poor previous experience of leadership are likely to elect a person who is self-centred, opportunistic and overconfident. This is because under conditions of stress or hardship, people erroneously take these attributes as an index for strength, determination and unwavering commitment. Such a phenomenon is rather more prevalent in instances of electing leaders and parties to power, than in the workplace. But in both scenarios, the biggest danger is that this change in one's personality takes place imperceptibly, often unknown to oneself.

Taken to an extreme, it leads to megalomania. But long before one ever gets to that stage, a sense of entitlement creeps into the mindset of leaders in privileged positions. They begin to echo the self-deluding belief: *The rules that apply to others, lesser mortals, don't apply to me.*[7] Apart from a psychological explanation for this phenomenon, there is a neurological aspect to it as well. The question then arises: If our very bodies and brains are wired to a behaviour of insensitivity that accompanies power, what hope, if any, is there of remedying it?

The answer lies, first and foremost, in self-awareness. This attribute is fundamental in that it makes a person realize that he is not infallible and enables him to be receptive to self-examination, advice and even criticism. Self-awareness is the stepping stone to any introspection and subsequent course correction. There are always those little checks and balances that can temper a leader's arrogance, and the most effective of these come in the form of candid feedback from his circle of trusted friends and colleagues.

Yet, typically, people are apprehensive of voicing their concerns for fear of retaliation, and so the leader continues in this fashion, till sometimes it is too late.

Power, Integrity and Empathy

Lord John Dalberg-Acton, the nineteenth-century English writer, historian and politician, famously stated: 'Power tends to corrupt and absolute power corrupts absolutely.' More than a century later, social scientists and psychologists are proving that in most cases, this dictum is correct. From tyrannical monarchs and military dictators to industry tycoons—history is replete with individuals lured by power to commit acts that are not just illegal and unethical but which have wide-ranging impact, far beyond their immediate spheres of influence. In our times, especially in an Indian corporate context, we need look no further than the well-chronicled 'dreams to riches to ashes' tale of Ramalinga Raju.[8]

Hailing from a rural, farming background, Raju was a self-made man with a grand dream—to build a corporate empire that would operate out of more than fifty countries and provide employment to more than 50,000 people. With this vision in mind, in 1987, he founded Satyam Computer Services in Secunderabad, with an initial employee strength of twenty. Over the next two decades, the trajectory of his company's rise was dream-like: establishing new centres, recruiting thousands of young professionals each year and acquiring an ever-growing list of clientele, including many of the global Fortune 500 companies.

Raju's vision soon transcended the running of a successful global business. Not content with the phenomenal growth of his company, he ventured into philanthropy in 2001, setting up the Byrraju Foundation, with an aim to building progressive self-reliant rural communities. Raju had become an iconic figure, adored by employees and investors, and respected by clients and competitors alike. But inside, the rot had begun to set in.

In January 2009, Raju shocked the corporate world by confessing that the company's accounts had been falsified. Through the course of the ensuing CBI investigation and trial, the sheer scale of the fraud came to light—a whopping $1.47 billion. The company had been reporting an employee headcount of 53,000 people, whereas the correct number was around 40,000; in effect, Raju had been withdrawing $3 million every month to pay 13,000 non-existent employees.

The scandal had far-reaching effects. Many of Satyam's largest clients severed their relationship; the company's stocks plummeted; and major stock exchanges stopped trading the company's shares. Satyam was stripped of its corporate awards and accolades and the image of Indian enterprise, in particular that of IT services, took a beating in the eyes of the world. After a very lengthy and involved investigation, on 9 April 2015, Raju and nine others were convicted of inflating the company's revenue, falsifying accounts and income-tax returns, criminal conspiracy, breach of trust and forgery, and were sentenced to a heavy fine and seven years' imprisonment. Ironically, Raju had named his organization 'Satyam', which, literally translated from Sanskrit, means 'truth'.

So, what prompted this man, who had shown such promise and enterprise, someone who enjoyed such adulation from the industry, to take recourse to nefarious means? Our surmise is that Raju's downfall came about because he betrayed the very principles based on which he first set up his company. He compromised his integrity, and having reached, in his own estimation, a supreme unimpeachable position, began to feel he was free to do anything and that no one could hold him accountable.

Integrity involves self-regulation and is closely tied to emotional intelligence. Often, the bad things that take place in companies are a result of impulsive behaviour on the part of its leader—an opportunity presents itself, and people with low impulse control simply say yes to it. One lie leads to another and eventually, the cover-ups snowball to a disaster of mammoth proportions. In Raju's own words: 'It was like riding a tiger, not knowing how to get off without being eaten.'

Contrast this with another true account, told by a friend of ours.

The Unexpected Guest—Viji Philip's Story

This was during the time I worked at Mindtree. I'd been with the company for a while and though things had been going okay, I had begun to look for opportunities outside the firm. I found one and put in my papers. It was a day like any other, except that I had just tendered my resignation. The family was sitting down to dinner, when the doorbell rang. I looked at my wife—were we expecting anyone? No, she said. I got up to answer the door. Imagine my utter surprise when I saw the man who was standing there—Subroto Bagchi, the MD of Mindtree!

He realized it was late, but he just wanted a quick word; would that be all right? But of course! The fact of seeing him at my doorstep didn't sink in at first. He came in, greeted the family, sat down and told me that he had seen my resignation mail. He said that he appreciated that there may be a personal imperative for me to look for a change and that, as a professional, he respected that.

However, he wished to know if there was anything in particular about the company I didn't appreciate, which prompted this decision on my part. Alternatively, was there anything specific that I felt could be improved, including any ideas or opportunities that might induce me to reconsider my decision? If so, he'd be happy to discuss it with me. Touched, flattered, and still astonished, I promised to think about it.

If this gesture on Mr Bagchi's part was amazing, what followed was no less so. Over the course of the following week, at multiple points, he took time off his incredibly busy schedule to sit with me and discuss various aspects of the company, my experience in it thus far and explore ideas through which I could contribute to the firm's success in a more meaningful and visible way. That interaction with Subroto Bagchi changed the very prism through which I had previously perceived leadership. For me, even today, he epitomizes the empathetic leader—his integrity, empathy and

> attention to the aspirations of individual employees make him clearly stand out as a role model.

Happily, this is not an isolated instance. Today, there is growing acceptance of the fact that a more congenial working environment leads to a motivated and therefore more productive workforce. This, to a large extent, reflects leadership style as well as what we call 'company culture'. Consequently, a growing number of leaders around the world are working proactively to change their image and adopt a softer, more pro-employee stance in communications and business dealings.[9]

Microsoft's Bill Gates transformed not only his organization but also his image to the outside world.[10] Right from the earliest days, when as a twenty-year-old, he co-founded Microsoft with Paul Allen, Gates took advantage of every opportunity to take his company to unprecedented, dominant heights. But this hegemony came under serious threat when in May 1998, the US Department of Justice filed a suit against Microsoft, accusing him of abusing Microsoft's monopoly power on Intel-based personal computers in its handling of operating system and web browser sales. At the trial, Gates's demeanour was both patronizing and pugnacious. Microsoft's market capitalization diminished considerably; Gates's stronghold on the domain broke; and his own persona in public imagination became tarnished to that of an arrogant, over-competitive corporate magnate.

Gates's course-correction was remarkable. He strategically scaled down the company's operations, stepped down as the CEO and, together with his wife Melinda, set up a foundation dedicated to philanthropy—going from various charitable organizations around the world tackling problems such as poverty, education and infectious diseases, to scientific research programmes. Today, his image is more that of a leader with strong moral values and philanthropic passions. And because of the brand association between Bill Gates and his company, there is a reassessment of his company's image in the public eye.

Organizations and Ethos

For organizations to become more people-centred and enhance their overall emotional intelligence, we need to understand what is popularly known as company culture. While nearly everyone agrees that every organization has its own distinctive culture, which is important and has an impact on the workings of the organization, there isn't any consensus around exactly what company culture entails. Apart from the nuances associated with what different people understand by the term 'culture', the confusion is compounded by popular notions, which aren't necessarily borne out by facts.

One such belief is that company culture is a monolith—a unified whole that binds all employees in an organization to the same common values, ideas, practices and behaviour. This idea presupposes that (a) all employees within an organization think and act alike, conforming to the 'culture' espoused by that organization, and (b) that these values, beliefs, ideals do not change over time. However, research, established acts and even what we see around us in our daily lives support neither of these premises.[11]

Not only are the boundaries of organizations permeable, they are also evolving all the time, as companies continually react to market demands, economic conditions and globalization, shifts in customer taste, trends and expectations, advances in technology and unforeseen exigencies. In the process, an organization influences and is in turn influenced by other companies, people and events.

There has also been a shift in our thinking. Since the 1980s, academics have been speaking of culture in terms of a process, as compared to something static. It is well established that corporates and institutions have aspirations, goals and philosophies, which they drive by means of specific processes and initiatives. But all the people working in these organizations do not necessarily share the same values. The common interpretation of 'company culture' is thus misleading.

A second, equally widespread notion is that company culture is only driven top-down by executives, who are generally intractable when it comes to embracing change or sourcing ideas from juniors;

and, consequently, that company culture is not employee-focused. However, the operations of large corporates today go well beyond the geopolitical boundaries of continents, impacting people (both employees and customers) who come from diverse backgrounds in terms of history, climate, race, cuisine, beliefs, traditions, practices and habits. In such a scenario, the values, traditions and aspirations of organizations are often calibrated to recognize and make space for diversity.

In the book *Reimagining India: Unlocking the Potential of Asia's Next Superpower*, Kumar Mangalam Birla, chairman of the Aditya Birla group, recounts his experience, when in 2003, in the wave of global expansion, his company acquired a copper mine in Australia.[12] Historically, the leaders of the family-run Aditya Birla group of companies had always been staunch traditionalists, from their corporate values to matters of creed, beliefs and practices, right down to the cuisine they preferred. No meat was served in company cafeterias; likewise, no alcohol offered at company functions.

This choice of cuisine, however, presented a real problem to Australian employees, who were concerned at having to forego what was, after all, part of their staple diet. The matter was settled as the new Birla management allowed their Australian employees to continue with the cuisine they were habituated to. However, what Mr Birla did not expect was a similar request from employees in India—and this is exactly what happened.

More and more Birla employees in India were asking why they should have to go meatless at parties, if employees abroad did not. It was a pretty valid point, yet one that had not struck the management as pertinent previously. On the one hand, the whole matter of non-vegetarian food went contrary to the traditional values of the Birlas. On the other, this demand represented the legitimate wishes of employees who came from communities observing different customs and habits, including food habits!

What swayed the matter in favour of an inclusive decision was this realization, in Mr Birla's words: 'Our company had to change with the times. If we wanted to make our mark on the world, we had to be prepared for the world to leave its mark on us.' This experience took him through a whole journey of realizations. Although unrelated to the company's core business, it nevertheless had a material impact on the daily lives of employees working in the company.

It also led him to an important conclusion:

> If you want all your employees to share the same values and to feel a sense of kinship with one another, as we do, you've got to work at creating an emotional bond ... treat all your employees and managers, Indian and non-Indian, equally. The views of people outside India have to count as much as those of people here at home. What's even more difficult for a tradition-bound company like ours, but just as valuable, is learning and importing values from the new acquisitions ... But the effort is worth it.

Far from being a monolith, the cultures that prevail across communities even within India are so complex, so finely nuanced and richly textured that very often we ourselves don't fully appreciate the full range of diversity in it. And rather than grand designs, sometimes, relatively small incidents help in sensitizing us to the specific needs of people we work with. Here's one such account.

A Question of Faith—Avik's Story

> One of the projects I was managing in the 2014-2015 time frame required my team to work full-time out of the client's offices. The project lead informed me that one of the team members, Shireen (name changed), was infrequent in attending meetings towards the back end of the week. Her motivation level and performance were also somewhat inconsistent. Given that the project deadlines required nothing less than full commitment from all team members, my initial reaction was to roll off Shireen. However, on second thoughts, I told my project lead to hold off, as I was planning to visit the client the next day. I decided to have a chat with Shireen.

> During my one-on-one meeting with her, she asked if she could work from home on Fridays, but under the given circumstances, that wasn't possible. She then asked if it would be possible to roll her off and have her work on any other engagement, based out of our offshore delivery centre. On investigating further, I learnt that Shireen's problem was that the client premises didn't have a separate prayer room, which made things difficult on Fridays, as she had to go out to a mosque (and there was none nearby) for the afternoon prayers, causing her to sometimes miss afternoon meetings. Over time, this led to a situation where a lot of anxiety built up in her as the week progressed, and she was hesitant to bring this up.
>
> Suddenly, I was able to connect the dots! We spoke to the client, and arranged things so that a conference room was booked through Friday afternoons, where she could offer prayers.

It is important to remember that whether as a team member or manager, executive or new joinee, each one of us is a potential catalyst for organizational change. Any company's culture is the complex product of the mindset of various individuals and interactions between them. But in order to make ourselves successful as catalysts, what we need is to be more open in our interactions with others, and thereby foster a culture of candour and transparency.

Many corporates today are seized of the need to make their policies more employee-friendly. From basketball courts and gyms within the premises to flexible hours and work-from-home options and making the evaluation process more transparent, there is greater investment in manpower and resources, to address the needs of employees. Both the authors of this book have worked in leading global consulting firms, where annual questionnaires and surveys ascertain what is working well in the company, as well as areas of concern that ought to be addressed.

Google is another good example.[13] The company uses a tool called Googlegeist to conduct an annual internal survey of all its employees. It covers aspects such as innovation and autonomy, forward thinking, teamwork and everything else considered important to the DNA of the culture. As John Kaplan, vice president of US sales and operations at Google, explains: 'We look at the suggestions received from our employees and analyse it every single year, and then we actually take every piece of feedback ... where we need to improve, and, over the course of the rest of the year, all of our programmes are designed to address the areas of our Googlegeist feedback that have not performed very well.'

Recognizing the need for change and acting on it are imperatives not just at the level of individuals and companies, but also at the macroeconomic level, changing the way people around the world perceive it. Countries such as South Korea, for instance, have traditionally had a hierarchical, conservative culture. Today, however, the picture looks different.[14] Companies are realizing that their continued success, both at home and internationally, requires an overhaul of the working culture, including aspects such as meetings to be kept to half an hour, no exclusive lifts for managers, cuts in bonus for bosses who don't take the stipulated holidays. The wheels of change are in motion.

Teams without Boundaries

There is another factor, intrinsically linked with cultures, that deepens the need for emotional maturity at work—and that is globalization. This phenomenon has brought to the fore the urgency for a genuine understanding of and respect for cultural differences. Experience tells us that collaboration across geographies and cultures is seamless only if there is a two-way understanding and empathy. Studies confirm that for global teams, physical separation and cultural differences are aspects that need to be carefully and sensitively addressed. If not well-managed, they can very easily create social distance or lack of emotional connection, which then leads to misunderstandings and mistrust.[15]

In such situations, the teams that are not within that circle of power typically begin the project with an innate sense of being disadvantaged. As the engagement progresses, and decisions are taken 'out there', i.e. onsite, and merely communicated to the other teams, the feeling turns to a sense of not being empowered. People in the other geographies are less inclined to speak up during meetings and conference calls, to voice their opinions, concerns and original viewpoints. From here, it is but a few steps to mistrust and resentment. Without an honest attempt to understand cultural nuances, the project will soon run into severe problems.

Admittedly, attuning oneself to the nuances of another culture is a complex skill, which takes time, perseverance, adaptability and even imagination. These inherent challenges aren't something we are trained or prepared for. Personality also has a part to play here, certain people adapt easier than others. In a global, cross-cultural environment, the primary difficulty one faces is that one's experience in 'reading' emotions and intent through words and expressions in one's own culture doesn't fit when it comes to other cultures.

Andy Molinsky is an expert in advising professionals to adapt to other cultures. In his view, we can often detect genuine motivation just by seeing the fire in their eyes or the passion in their voice. This ability, however, is limited to the culture that we are most familiar with, and does not necessarily hold when we cross over to other cultures and venture into a completely different world of emotional expression. Emotions vary tremendously across cultures—both in terms of expression and meaning. Without a detailed understanding of these emotional landscapes, crossing cultures can feel like stepping into a communication minefield.[16]

And with the addition of each new team that belongs to a different geography/culture combination, the overall complexity in the interaction between the individual teams increases manifold. You may be part of the offshore team based in India, with the headquarters of the client in the US. However, this may be a global project that the company is undertaking, across the Americas, Europe, Middle East and Asia Pacific.

Accordingly, the overall project team consists of team members from countries as different from each other culturally as France and Korea, Germany and Brazil. For a leader or project manager of such an engagement, therefore, what is required is a full map of cross-cultural perspectives.[17] The big question here is—if navigating the cultural map is so incredibly complex, how does one actually go about it?

First, we need to figure out what the cultural norms are in those other geographies and how they differ from the home culture in directness, enthusiasm, formality, and so forth. For example, German people may exhibit certain behaviours or responses to a given situation which are very different from those of the Chinese. Learning and understanding those codes of conduct is the first step in working across cultures.

But just the knowledge of cultural nuances doesn't always help us adapt. For that, we have to practise new behaviours in actual situations and that requires us to step out of our cultural comfort zone. This takes time, patience, perseverance and a real passion to truly understand people. And once we know what adaptations we need to make, we need to keep practising them, till they become routine, natural or, in scientific terms, 'muscle memory'.[18]

Bowing in Korea—Suman's story

Before relocating to Korea for my work stint, I had read up on Korean culture and realized how different it was from our Indian culture. I learnt that people in the workplace showed respect to their seniors by bowing. Armed with that knowledge, although unsure if it were something I would be comfortable doing, I landed in Korea.

On observing people closely at work, I noticed the different nuances that the guide book had not equipped me with, which were real eye-openers. For instance, the way people bowed and the extent to which they bent forward varied based on the hierarchic position of the person they were bowing to. So, was I to emulate that behaviour to show perfect understanding and respect for the local culture, or by doing so, did I actually run the risk of offending my seniors by not doing it correctly?

I pondered over this question and also discussed it with some of my Korean and American colleagues whom I was close to. Eventually, I settled for an in-between solution—I decided not to do a similar bow but would convey my respect to my elders by a slight but definite nod of the head while maintaining eye contact. This approach balancing diversity and respect was well received by my Korean management.

When the cultural differences within a team are huge, it helps to minimize some of those differences by homogenizing things, by deploying uniform tools, methods, templates for work products and so forth, all the way up to the protocol for communication. However, sometimes, organizations are tempted to use this approach as the full solution. In other words, they believe that if teams across geographies adopt uniform tools, methods, templates for work products and even the protocol for communication, cultural differences can be brushed aside.

Our own take on this is that cultural nuances do matter, as does the history whereby these cultures have developed over time. You may be part of the offshore team of a large global project, with a uniform code of project standards, templates and documentation. But essentially, you're still in India, where there are scorching hot summers, spicy curries, people conversing in different languages and often wearing their emotions where their cufflinks ought to be. In fact, we feel that it is this very richness of distinctions and textures that gives rise to healthy debate, creative ideas and innovative solutions and services. And for the businesses of today, innovation is almost synonymous with survival.

The Constant Search for 'New'

Across industries and sectors, product life cycles are shrinking rapidly. There is pressure on companies to continually launch new products, while lowering prices on older models or versions, managing the inventory for the same and eventually phasing them out. Mobile phones are a case in point. Automobiles are another, wherein even premium brands are not an exception. Mercedes Benz India, for example, had a '15 in '15' strategy, which saw them launching fifteen models in 2015.

This shows that both product and service organizations need to constantly keep abreast of evolving customer requirements, maintain a high level of creativity and retain the agility to launch products to market faster than their competitors. Innovation is thus critical for organizations today. While several organizations have woken up to this reality, the actual process of adapting to make this happen is proving to be quite hard.

This requires a fundamental change in the way many companies still think and do business. They cut across every facet of an organization—not just in revamping systems and structures and policies, but bringing about a shift in behaviours and mindsets. For innovation to be truly successful, it needs to be everyone's job, in the same way that maintaining quality is the job of everybody in the team, and not limited to just a few individuals in R&D earmarked for 'innovation initiatives'.

Some organizations have begun adopting a set of principles revolving around better understanding of customer needs, by building empathy with customers and then iterating with them to get a better product or application, in order to reduce time to market. This approach, known as Design Thinking, is now gaining currency with enterprises worldwide. The starting point of innovation is not just imagination but empathy. We think with our heads but buy with our hearts. Which is why the products with the most features don't necessarily win over a market. Pure technical innovations that fail to create holistic, emotional experiences for consumers are not likely to be big hits.[19]

However, empathy and business imperatives do not always go hand in hand. Organizations sometimes focus more on the cognitive and rational aspects rather than the emotional. We look at a typical press statement or website and see words like 'execution', 'focus' and 'differentiation'. There is nothing wrong with these words, except that they don't inspire us or touch our hearts. They are driven by an ethos that runs counter to empathy, because at the end of the day, people working in organizations need to be inspired and customers need to have that 'feel-great' factor, when they're buying a product or availing a service. Which again is all about the way companies can appeal to their emotions.[20]

Having empathy for customers requires company strategists to step out of their comfort zone and meet the world outside, fraught with uncertainty, unexpected findings, difficult people or situations. This is the place to find insights and understand real needs.[21] Unless this happens, organization leaders develop the tendency to become insular and inward-looking. So, there's a need to shift from hard-nosed financials towards subjective aspects of innovation. Organizations that 'get' design use words such as desires, aspirations, engagement and experience to describe products and users. Here, emotionally charged language isn't seen as flaky, silly or 'not data-driven'.[22]

After gaining insights from the real world, the next step is to build a working model with which we can interact with our customers. We continue building more prototypes and/or improving the current ones to quickly arrive at meeting customer needs. This iterative process can have setbacks along the way. But even those small failures are useful because they show what works and what needs change. This ability to 'fail forward' is a critical component of innovation and, behaviourally, it requires a mindset where one is comfortable with failure and can learn from it. Innovation warrants a departure from 'getting it right the first time', as each prototype is by definition incomplete. It requires courage and vulnerability to place these prototypes before critical customers.[23]

The table below summarizes typical external dynamics at play in today's global business workplace—what they mean for an organization and how they can be addressed through emotional intelligence.

External change	What it means internally for an organization	How to bring that change in the context of EQ
Borderless world – news travels fast and wide	Be ethical	- Self-awareness, impulse control
	Be planet-focused	- Transparency, sustainability
	Treat people well	- Engage and empower employees
		- Be an empathetic leader
		- Safeguard against Power Paradox
Globalization	Cultural sensitivity	- Understand and practise new behaviours to cater to other cultures
		- Balance 'company culture' with individual needs
Rapidly changing customer needs	Be innovative	- Gain deeper insights through empathetic listening, Design Thinking
Changing demographics	Integrate 'old-timers' with 'newcomers'	- Navigate tectonic shifts, e.g., generational shifts
		- Change company culture to cater to changed demographics and environment (e.g., millennials)
Hyper-competition	Manage high cost pressures	- Multidimensional skills
		- Be realistic and reflective

Figure 3.4: EQ adaptation to external changes

Continuous and successful innovation implies a high emotional quotient in areas such as conflict management, communication and collaboration. It requires constructive conflict—to be able to allow intense debates and points of view, so that no new ideas are killed upfront, even while not allowing the debates to get personal. Innovative ideas and initiatives need to be enabled by high-quality communication and collaboration, requiring a mental shift away from competition. This is even more critical for 'open innovations', where ideas can flow from outside the enterprise, from other companies and industries.

In this chapter, we have focused on the main factors that explain why the complex, changing and challenging dynamics of today's workplace actually underscore the need for greater emotional enablement. There is another aspect: the increasing proportion of younger people joining the workforce; their expectations, wishes and aspirations; the way they are perceived by leaders; and the eternal inter-generation clash played out anew, in a Digital Age. And this is the subject of our next chapter.

4

How Do You Manage the Millennials?

Life Decisions over Breakfast

The company boasts of having the best corporate cafeteria in the country. While the airy ambience of the place encourages co-workers to 'hang out', the menu on offer can easily vie with some of the better restaurants in town. Breakfast by itself is a sumptuous feast. And Mohan, who has logged in early and is famished by now, fancies an English-style meal, with eggs to order. Nitin gets a plate of parathas.

A year back, the two friends joined this enviably happening firm, straight out of campus. They've been working in different teams and their meal-time tête-à-têtes are a nice way for them to catch up on what's happening in their lives, at the workplace and beyond. But this morning, things are rather special.

'So ...' Nitin asks, 'have you made a decision?'

'Yeah ... I've given it a lot of thought, and like we both keep saying, this is a cool place ... but I've learnt all I had to, at my current level...'

'Yes, in your area, perhaps, but what about other domains...'

'Even if I shift to another team, the learning curve there will run its course in two or three months ... and then what? Know what I mean?'

'OK ... so what do you want to do?'

'See, man, I'm interested in figuring out the real drivers behind businesses that run successfully, what really makes things tick, you know, as opposed to doing things mechanically. I want to advise people, strategize…'

'But that only comes with experience.'

'Experience … but also, the right kind of training!' Mohan, who has food in his mouth, cups a hand over it, waiting till it goes down. 'And don't get me wrong, I've been getting some solid experience here. But what I want to do now is to study, get an MBA from a top school and then join a firm like, say, McKinsey. And who knows … I could come back to this very place someday, but as an advisor, to help with their strategy, not do more of the same legwork.'

'You are going to miss this place, then?'

'Oh, no question about it, Nitin! This is a great place to work in. But like I told you earlier, once you have a different long-term goal, it's better to take the decision sooner rather than later, and work towards it. All right … enough about me, yaar, how are things at your end? What you're planning is far more exciting.'

'Not so sure about *exciting*. Being in the civil service is something that has always interested me … and where I'm from, yeah, it's like the done thing. And anyway, it'll be great to be with my family for a while, and enjoy the home-cooked food!'

'Ah, now I understand the real motivation.' Mohan laughs.

'No … but seriously, if you see, a shift like this is really not that rare. Remember Pradeep, from two batches earlier? He did a very similar thing, joined one of the Big Four consulting firms, had two years of experience, wrote his exams, got through … he'll be starting his training soon, in Ghaziabad.'

Their food wolfed down by now, they glance at their watches and nod at each other. Time to head back. But also, a pact of sorts has been made, regarding their future life direction.

The Old Order Changeth…

Millennials! The very mention of this term can evince (depending on the context and demographics of those in question) a wide spectrum of feelings, from a sense of enthusiasm, pride and identity to that of incomprehensibility, scepticism and unease—and just about everything in between. In fact, anything but apathy.

The millennial debate has dominated discussions in many HR and corporate forums, both in India and abroad. Champions and critics of this dynamic, WhatsApp-addicted, gadget-toting, social media–dependent generation are already sharply defined. And in certain workplace situations it's as if invisible battlelines have been drawn—between the millennials, full of hope and energy as well as a sense of entitlement and facing a bar of expectations from others that's set quite high, and the people whom they typically report to, the 'oldies' who've worked their way into being part of the leadership group and who don't really seem to understand them. But one thing is for certain—this new generation simply cannot be ignored.

The millennials, i.e., those born between 1980 and 2000, are forming an increasing proportion of today's workforce as well as customer base around the world, a trend that will only continue and predominate in the years to come. According to the PwC survey[1] report on millennials, this cohort already forms 25 per cent of the workforce in the US and accounts for over half of the population in India. The projection is that by 2020, millennials will form 50 per cent of the global workforce. No surprise then that the outlook, aspirations and attitudes to work of this new generation are expected to have a significant impact on work culture.

Thus, for a growing majority of organizations across the world, the ability to attract and retain top talent from the millennial generation emerges as a key strategic imperative. Retention has a lot to do with making them settle in, assimilating them seamlessly into the existing workforce structure. A key factor in making this integration successful is the genuine two-way understanding between the millennials and the older generation in the workplace. Which in turn underscores the importance of emotional enablement.

As the writers of this book, we can speak for ourselves. During the course of our careers, both of us have had occasion to work closely with millennials, in groups as well as in an individual capacity, in India and also abroad. Our experience has been wide and varied, from the instructional (be that tech-savvy or being informed about trends, there's much to learn from the younger generation), innervating (the sheer level of energy among millennials is remarkable, and contagious) to instances of bewilderment (although we may be talking the same language, there's still some disconnect between what we're each saying). But it's undeniable that close interactions with the younger generation have improved our awareness about them, and helped us to become better users of technology!

An interesting and widely debated point in the whole discourse about millennials is whether they are changing the workplace or actually being changed by it. But before we delve into that debate, it may be useful to explore the ways in which millennials are truly unique from earlier generations, and whether, in the final analysis, they are all that different.

After all, the term 'generation gap' has been around for quite a while, certainly predating the millennial generation. And all of us, regardless of which generation we belong to, would have at some point of time or other in our lives felt that we're not really understood by the older folks, and with it, however subliminal, has crept in the sense that things need to change, and that we will be the ones to bring about that change.

One is reminded of the lines from Tennyson's famous poem 'On the Passing of Arthur', which has been in vogue for well over a century, familiar to some of us as a text studied in our schooldays:

> The old order changeth, yielding place to new,
> And God fulfils himself in many ways,
> Lest one good custom should corrupt the world.[2]

Even in this poem, written well over a hundred years ago, the inevitability of change, accompanied by a sense of the younger order 'taking over' is unmistakable. But isn't that essentially true for each successive generation? And haven't their life experiences (in some countries and cultures more than in others) been quite different from those of the preceding generation?

While there certainly are attributes that set millennials apart, research shows that this is perhaps not more than can be explained by means of a generational difference, a cognitive bias, as opposed to genuine differences. And perceptions that older people carry may not be necessarily true. Peter Cappelli, George W. Taylor professor of management at the Wharton School, has extensively researched this topic and his view is: 'It's easy to assume younger people are different in disposition because they seem different from you. But young people are always different from older people ... for example, they don't have obligations in the same way older people do.'[3]

Flippant descriptions of millennials characterize them as being easily distracted, lazy, self-absorbed, entitled, ambitious and narcissistic. However, such perceptions are not confirmed by empirical research. On the contrary, studies suggest that employees of all ages are more alike than different in their attitudes at the workplace.

Researchers at George Washington University and the Department of Defence, having analysed twenty such studies, concluded with the words—'meaningful differences among generations probably do not exist at the workplace.' A 2015 national study commissioned by CNBC came to the same conclusion. On analysing key traits in potential employers, such as work–life balance, reputation, ethics and environmental practices, it was found that millennial preferences were about the same as those of the broader population.[4]

Every generation follows observable historical patterns and thus offers an empirical tool for predicting as well as analysing future trends. As Neil Howe and William Strauss put it, every new generation 'is shaped by events or circumstances according to which phase of life its members occupy at the time. As each generation ages into the next phase—from youth to young adulthood to midlife to elderhood—its attitudes and behaviours mature, producing new currents in the public mood'.[5]

One method of ascertaining the true distinctions in values, aspirations and attitudes of millennials is to explore the differences between earlier generations and their predecessors. And in doing so, the first thing that one realizes is that each generation, regardless of its geographic or cultural setting, is to a large extent a product of its times.

Consider, in the case of India, the generation that grew up during the 1950s and '60s, in a free, democratic country for the first time in over two centuries, enjoying the fruits of Independence. Although today we may take such things for granted, reflect on how crucial self-determination is. The basic right to vote. This was the generation that educated and established themselves gradually, through years of perseverance and hard work, till they came to a point when they could call themselves the proud owners of a TV set, a two-wheeler, or even a car!

Weren't the lives of these people and the values shaped thereby fundamentally different from those of their parents, who had seen oppression, deprivation and discrimination during British rule? Weren't their attitudes and expectations, including those at the workplace, significantly different?

Now consider the following generation, those who grew up in the '70s. Opportunities for education and work, and therefore of shaping one's future, were far greater in comparison to what their parents had. Riding the crest of liberalization, economic prosperity and the IT revolution, this was also the first generation in post-Independence India which got the opportunity to interact with people across the globe. Another significant trend has been the rising number of women (across the world, but very noticeably in India) joining the workforce and succeeding as professionals.

For this generation, over the course of time, cable TV and the Internet, computers and cell phones, all came to be essentials of daily life. From here, just another generation on—and we have the millennials! Culturally, socially, economically—it may seem like light years from the days of the Raj, but all this transformation has occurred in the span of just half a century.

Are the millennials a different species altogether, then? Perhaps not.

So What Sets the Millennials Apart?

From a historiographical perspective, especially when equated with the experience of previous generations vis-à-vis that of their predecessors, the millennials as a distinct entity may seem less stark.

Having said that, there are several distinctive factors about them that one needs to consider, especially with regard to integrating them with the older groups in the workforce, motivating them and making the most of their talent and potential.

Multiple jobs, multiple lives: Recall the conversation between Mohan and Nitin at the beginning of this chapter. Although they had joined a prestigious company that believes in taking care of its employees, a year down the line both of them are eager for a change. And what's equally important, it's possible that they may not stick to the new job, domain or even industry for the rest of their working lives.

Mohan may well go on to form his own consulting firm or a start-up while Nitin, having gained experience as an administrator, may set up his own NGO, or become a writer, or pursue these or other projects parallel with his day job as a bureaucrat. For millennials, the emphasis is on exploring multiple opportunities and openings, not on sticking to one's comfort zone.

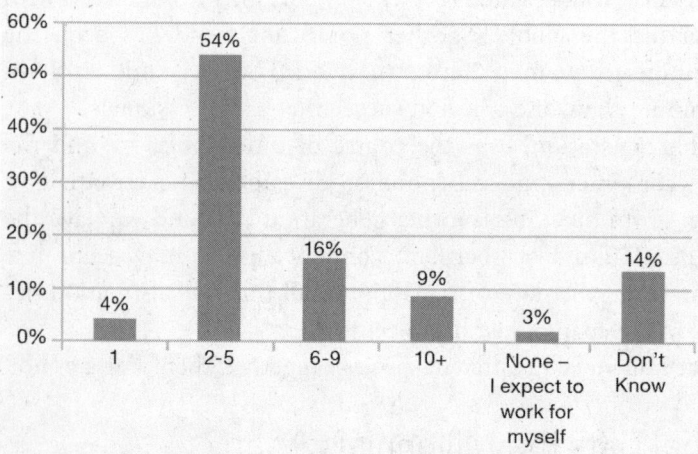

Figure 4.1: Job-changing preference of millennials

Such a career approach may be attributed to various factors, including the following:

- The choices and opportunities available to young professionals today is far greater and more varied than was available to professionals of an earlier generation.
- They have grown up in a competitive environment with a high degree of peer pressure, and are confident of their ability to succeed, even if they venture into something new.
- This approach of multi-careerism or holding several jobs at once may also stem from economic necessity, as having multiple attributes and skills (to match multiple selves) make it easier to earn a living; this also indicates that millennials as a group are more adept at assuming a particular form of self or role, as well as switching between several such, in ways earlier generations would find completely baffling, if not alien.[6]
- The way that millennials, brought up on playbooks and Xbox, view or approach life is significant, and increases one's risk-taking appetite and the urge to broaden one's horizon and sphere of experience. According to a study at MTV in 2011, as high a proportion as 50 per cent of the respondents said they viewed 'real life as a video game'.[7]

Technology and social interaction: Millennials thrive on technology. Addiction to games, gadgets and social media, listening to music on iPhones while at work, and preferring email exchanges to a whole lot of phone calls are the norm with them. A study at Adobe found that a whopping 98 per cent of millennials check their personal emails several times during the workday, while an almost equally high 87 per cent turn to work-related emails beyond working hours.[8]

While many corporate leaders still advocate the dictum: 'Get off the email-chain, pick up the phone and talk', this does not always translate into action on the ground, and millennials, according to many experts[9], as well as in our personal experience, abhor phone calls, particularly long ones. In fact, across several organizations, business calls and teleconferences are on the decline. And it is the younger cohort in the workforce that is leading this change.

This excessive techno-centric approach, not just to work, but to all aspects of life is something that naturally perplexes the older generation. The preponderance of phones, tablets and other devices may well be a cause of distraction for their users; however, it is equally possible that this distracts older members of the workforce, who are unused to such devices. Millennials who have mastered the art of processing multiple simultaneous message flows (e.g., music on the iPhone, WhatsApp messages and the ongoing work on the laptop screen) are generally able to multitask well.

And there is a science behind this as well. Millennials survive on social sharing, whether discussing work, narrating what happened at the team party or showing off their newest acquisition. Neuroscientists have demonstrated that positive interaction with other people gives us a high. This is because such an interaction lights up that part of the brain called the temporoparietal junction, which in turn stimulates the production of the feel-good hormone, oxytocin. But in the case of millennials, the same 'high' is reached by Facebook likes, Twitter posts, forwards, sharing and complimentary comments through the course of the day.[10]

One fallout of this is the reduced interaction levels among millennials and between them and other age groups. In a culture where Twitter and text abbreviations abound and emojis are used in lieu of words expressing emotions and feelings, the number of conversations that millennial professionals have on an average during the day is significantly lower than that of their counterparts in higher age groups. There is a strong possibility, therefore, that when complex, in-person conversations are warranted, such as a difficult career conversation, millennials are not naturally equipped to handle those situations well.

In fact, in our conversations with millennials, there've been multiple instances where they came off such interactions with their immediate line managers feeling thwarted, confused, misunderstood or that they have not been able to get their point across. Given the complex demands on human interactions within and beyond the workplace, this is an area that needs greater attention.

Values and social responsibility: Each generation has its values, and for the millennials, social impact and responsibility are of paramount importance. Whether it comes to products of their choice or prospective employers, the younger cohort wants companies to demonstrate responsible social behaviour. Positive, tangible impacts on communities rank higher in their minds than increases in profit and shareholder value. They insist that concern for the environment as well as underprivileged sections of society should form a core part of corporates' strategic imperatives.

Impact investment—the idea that private capital can be directed to solving pressing social needs, while still allowing for financial profit—is a good case in point. According to 'Millennials and Money', a 2014 study from Merrill Lynch, millennials cite social impact as one of the most important roles of business. To that end, they are themselves quite likely to trade greater financial return for beneficial social impact. In fact, they are likely to use their investment preferences and choices as a statement, reflecting their social, political and environmental beliefs.[11]

A Morgan Stanley report reached a very similar conclusion: Millennials are twice as likely to endorse brands that have a good track record of social impact and sound environmental policies.[12] Financial houses such as BlackRock have now begun introducing funds specifically aimed at millennials. The fund seeks stocks that advance health, benefit the environment and treatment of workers.

Conversely, when companies are seen to wilfully mislead investors and customers, it has a deep adverse effect on millennials. Volkswagen is a case in point. The company tried to make people believe their cars were cleaner than they really were, and the results were disastrous.[13] Analysts call this 'clean-label investing'.

But the demand for this clean label goes beyond investing and buying of products, and impacts the decision-making of millennials with regard to employers. Research shows that this cohort is three times as likely, compared with the earlier generation, to seek employment with an organization based on its stance on social and/or environmental issues.[14] And corporates are taking serious cognizance of this.

As Bob Moritz, PwC chairman in the US, notes: 'When I was coming up, we didn't ask why we were doing it. We didn't give much thought to our role in society.' Had this been a generation ago, when he began his career, he would have been clearly astonished at the fact that 'PwC's millennials don't only demand to know the organization's purpose—its reason for being—but also are prepared to leave the firm if that purpose doesn't align with their own values.'[15]

In India, where large corporates employ tens of thousands of employees, this is no less critical. In HCL, which employs more than 87,000 people, the average age is twenty-eight. Vineet Nayar, vice chairman of the company, feels millennial workers raised on social media have special skills in pulling together solutions, and they know how to mobilize their networks. This ability to quickly collect and make sense of information and respond in real time often trumps experience. However, the younger cohort is sometimes not engaged enough, or committed enough, to contribute and make a difference on the ground. At HCL, Nayar is trying to bring about a better integration through measures such as a 360-degree appraisal and programmes such as Power of One, which allows employees to contribute time and energy to social causes.[16]

Motivation and self-absorption: Making allowances for exceptions in both the millennial cohort and its earlier generation, one feature distinguishing the two is what motivates employees most at the workplace. While with the earlier generation, it has largely been money and prospects of higher earnings, promotions and additional responsibilities, experts say that with millennials, the primary motivator is training and development—the acquisition of new skills and learning.[17]

They believe in 'following their passion'.[18] Their education and upbringing, the seemingly endless array of opportunities open to them, doting parents and peer-group solidarity have reinforced this sentiment over and over. Consequently, the approach is largely to focus on the areas of interest and then mapping a career path that fits with it. But there are two risks with this approach:

A. One's passions and interests change over time, and it is difficult to calibrate one's career accordingly, or 'course-correct' midstream, as the case might be.
B. There may be an inherent clash between one's passions and the ground reality, as experienced through opportunities available in the market; in case of a clash, the millennials inevitably suffer, as they then have to opt for openings that are a compromise, taking them away from their areas of interest.

A worrying implication of this, which has been vindicated by some studies,[19] is that millennials constantly crave challenge at the workplace and are bored and demotivated by routine work. While the previous generation may have sought some sort of comfort zone, however wide, in which to establish themselves, millennials seek to do new, different things at frequent intervals.

Falling into any kind of predictable pattern of work, activities and deliverables can swiftly become anathema, at which point they start to feel that they have very little to do or contribute in their jobs, or that their skills and talents are not being properly utilized.[20] The conversation between Mohan and Nitin that we saw earlier strikes a chord in this regard.

On analysing this distinction, it appears that at least some of it can be explained by a difference in what we call 'work ethic'.[21] In general terms, people in management, still largely comprising members of the older generation, tend to see the problem essentially as a manifestation of an inherent trait of laziness and disregard for protocol among young professionals.

A large majority of professionals in the older generation has matured on a regime of guidelines and procedures, and in the process, they are more willing to sacrifice 'work–life balance'. Many have traded in longer, unpredictable work schedules for promotions, raises and responsibilities, without necessarily questioning the fundamentals underlying the processes.

Millennials, on the other hand, demand a better work–life balance and flexibility in their schedules.[22] Time and a good level of control over it are both important to them, as is work–life balance. Therefore, scarcity of time irks them, as it disrupts their ability to balance work and their personal commitments.

During our interaction with millennials, this concept of 'me-time' has often come to the fore. But there could be another reason why personal time is important to them—because of their ceaseless quest for their own selves and their great need for sharing, chiefly through social media but also in person. People critical of the millennials have lampooned this as overriding narcissism. The extent to which this is true, or whether it is true, across a clear majority of millennials, is debatable.

However, we do feel there is a great deal of self-absorption, which fuels the constant need to share details about their lives. Since, for many millennials, the division between the strictly professional and personal spheres is blurred, it is not uncommon to have them share very personal details or to talk at length about their aspirations, problems and family dynamics even in a professional setting. Regardless of the term we choose to describe this trait, it tends to make them less effective team members in the workplace.[23]

Mentoring, feedback and collaboration: Another significant distinction for millennials is their relationship (as workforce) with management. For them, the old command-and-control style of management not only doesn't produce the best results, it can even be counterproductive. While the older generation has largely adhered to processes and instructions, millennials—equipped with (and therefore, far more dependent on) technology and mutual endorsement within the peer or friend circle—tend to question these processes and voice their own opinions.

Instead of following instructions from their line managers, they often need to be convinced that it is the right approach. Collaboration and mentoring, rather than military obedience, is the order of the day. While employees across all age groups would like to feel valued, empowered and engaged at work, millennials have taken this several steps ahead, from being a wish to a fundamental requirement.[24]

Mentoring becomes a particularly important component of what millennials in the workplace expect from bosses, mostly through the form of regular feedback, one-on-one conversations and informal catch-ups. While the need for mentoring varies across individuals and situations, the expectations from leadership are nuanced, multifarious and demanding. We categorize them as below:

- **Frequency:** According to studies, most millennials appreciate a regular cadence, such as monthly, although depending on the situation, the expectation is of more frequent conversations;[25] in our personal experience with some millennials, certain instances called for almost daily touchpoint.
- **Endorsement:** All of us like praise, but millennials appear to crave it more than earlier generations did; endorsements that seem generic or insincere, however, are immediately rejected; again, praise is more appreciated if a one-on-one exchange is complemented in a group or team situation, or in the form of performance awards.
- **Growth path:** Millennials expect that they will be provided a concrete roadmap by their leaders, along with tips on how to make them successful; the sense of fast-tracking one's career can be particularly strong, expressed through the question—how can I learn and grow faster? Respect for supervisors and leaders does not come with seniority, par for the course; rather, millennials need to be led from the front and inspired for them to have genuine respect and trust for their managers.

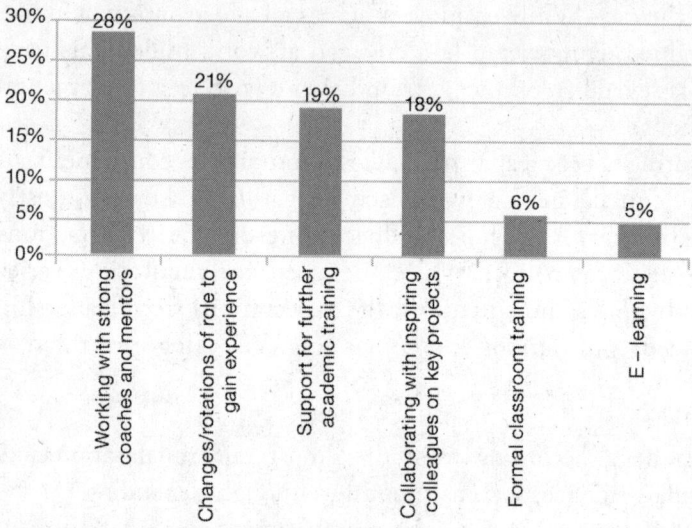

Figure 4.2: Millennials' expectations from employers

INSEAD's Emerging Markets Institute, Universum, and the Singapore-based think tank HEAD conducted a large annual survey of millennials, comprising over 16,000 people across Asia, Africa, Europe, Latin America, the Middle East and North America.[26] According to this survey, millennials felt that a good manager was one who empowers employees, is a technical or functional expert in the domain, sets transparent performance criteria and evaluates them objectively, assigns goal-oriented work and is a role model.

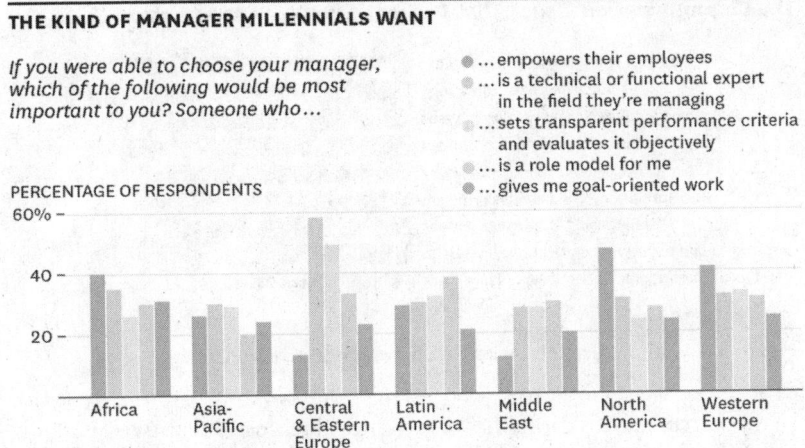

Figure 4.3: The kind of manager millennials want

- **Advice and criticism:** Feedback also needs to be constructive, and while advice and suggestions are welcome, feedback that is more critical is less so. And this brings us to an area of concern. Millennials feel empowered to voice their opinions, differences and also provide feedback to their leaders, a case in point being when an intern told Facebook founder Mark Zuckerberg that he needed to work on his public-speaking skills; not only was the intern hired, Zuckerberg actually worked on the feedback.[27]

Likewise, millennials are scathing when it comes to accusing leadership of a lack of emotional intelligence—from micromanagement to bullying—as a 2015 US survey of working millennials shows.[28]

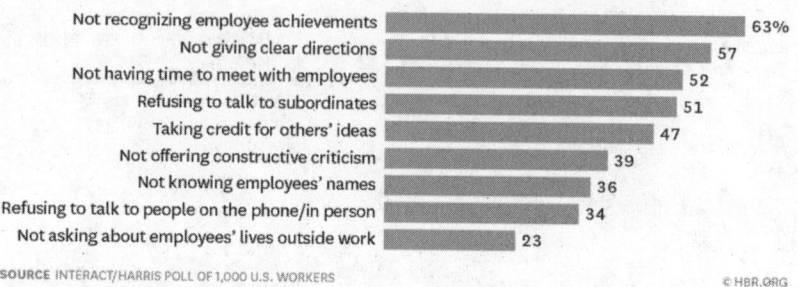

Figure 4.4: Communication issues that prevent effective leadership

In a converse situation, however, they are less receptive when it comes to accepting criticism and working on it; while a culture of endorsements and praise generally makes it harder for people to accept their own drawbacks, this may also be linked to the millennial trait of self-absorption and high degree of self-esteem.

Changing the Workplace—or Changed by It?

In the emerging literature on businesses and people, there is growing focus on millennials. Much of the press reports, while focusing on the same topic, are sensational, bordering on the downright apocalyptic. For instance, according to a *60 Minutes* story: 'A new breed of American worker is about to attack everything you hold sacred...'[29]

This is clearly an exaggeration. There are some experts who therefore feel that the effect of millennials itself is largely hype. While acknowledging changes such as increased proportion of women or adoption of technology in the workplace, they feel that overall, today's workplaces will change Gen Y more than the reverse.

The other school of thought points to the evidence around us: technology driving business more than ever before, an increased use of and conducting of business through mobile devices, the growing power of social media and the ever-rapid increase in the number of businesses and start-ups, such as Facebook, which are founded or led by millennials. There is even the hope that this cohort, with its insistence on better work–life balance, will change the workday back to a nine to five schedule.[30]

In India, there is now greater and concerted focus on makeovers at an organizational level, to match the new mindset and work ethic brought to the workforce by millennials. According to R. Chandrasekhar, president of NASSCOM: 'Digital is pervading everything … the momentum is increasing at a rapid pace, led by the fact that the workforce is increasingly constituted by those who joined after 2000.'[31] NASSCOM's summits in 2014 and 2015 have emphasized the need for better employee engagement and empowerment, as the salient points from their report show:

- Simplified work environments and practices
- Customized HR solutions that treat each employee individually
- Social media to drive democratization of work
- Investments in new and accelerated models to develop leaders at all levels
- Adapt to a global world, matching talent with tasks and supporting mobile workforces across geographies

In the light of our research and our personal interactions with millennials across geographies, our own views may be summarized as follows:

- The workplace of today is not a static environment, but the product of a complex mosaic of factors, including economic uncertainties and climatic shifts, changing customer tastes and disruptive technologies, to name only a few. In terms of the processes, work practices and technologies supporting businesses, the workplace today is substantially, if not completely, different from what it was a decade or two ago.

While this is largely true across all global economies, it is particularly so for India, which has witnessed tremendous technological and infrastructural development during this period. Therefore, over and above the debate in question, it would be accurate to say that millennials are entering a changed (and constantly changing) workplace.[32]

- We feel that with an ever-increasing number of millennial cohorts joining the workforce, it would be realistic to assume this would have at least some impact on the way businesses are conducted around the world. Organizations around the world are now talking of digitization and gamification; there is also a growing trend among large global corporates to do away with the 'bell-curve' performance rating system. The new imperative for CHROs is to 'recommend ways to use human capital to unlock or create value'.[33]

But how much of this is because of a 'Millennial Revolution', as compared with a general growing awareness of the need for better emotional enablement, as a means of employee engagement? Because there are so many factors changing today's workplace, and the changes themselves are so diverse, it is difficult to single out a direct causality of the change factors brought about by the millennials and the exact impact of the same on the workforce.

- To us, more important than whether or not millennials are changing the workplace (and if so, to what extent?) is the following question: Given that millennials will soon form the single largest cohort in the workforce, what steps are organizations taking to make the integration seamless and fruitful? These and other issues we will continue to discuss through the course of the book, especially in the later chapters.

5

From STEM to ESTEEM

Mastering the Forest

In medieval times, a Japanese warlord once sent his son to a Zen Master to further his education. An emissary carried a note that the elderly monk read in silence. 'Reverend Master,' said the letter, 'I present to you my only son. In his growing years, I had expected him to observe the qualities that will one day make him a custodian of his people. Instead, I find him undisciplined, lazy and haughty, and at this rate, he will come to naught. Therefore, I request you to place him under your tutelage and inculcate in him the values that will make him a true leader, no matter how long it takes. Give no thought to his lineage—be firm with him.'

The boy soon learnt that this monastery was not a place where he could expect any special privileges. He woke up at dawn to a day filled with prayer, lessons and tasks that back home he'd have considered too menial to bother with, interspersed with frugal meals, and at night, he slept on an uncomfortable, cold, hard bed. It was a life that epitomized discipline in practice. He had no choice but to follow the same routine as his fellow novitiates—or miss out on his food. Slowly, and with the greatest reluctance, he began to conform.

Time passed, and then the boy began to miss home and its comforts all over again. Also, he was bored. How long was this supposed toughening-up period going to last? Hadn't he been here long enough already? But no one from home had come to fetch him. And without the Master's permission, there was no question of him returning on his own.

So, one day, he came and stood before the Master and said: 'Holy sir, I have been here in the monastery several months now, living the hard life of a novitiate. I have observed the precepts and learnt the scriptures as well as any of the others have. What else is expected of me?' The Master remained silent. 'When can I go home?'

'When you have mastered the forest,' came the reply.

It wasn't the answer the boy was expecting. He nodded slowly, bowed and took his leave. Behind the monastery, the forest was an unbroken stretch into the distance, tapering off only where the mountains began their upward climb. The whole place was uninhabited, except for the wild animals that were said to prowl its depths. To the boy, the forest represented the harsh realities of the world, and as the son of a warlord, he reflected, he was naturally required to prove his mettle by braving its dangers. The test was therefore symbolic, and could be accomplished by spending a night in the forest, alone. Yes, that is what the Master must have meant. The boy plucked up courage, took his sword, some food and water, and went into the woods, returning to the monastery the following morning.

'What did you experience in the forest?' asked the Master.

The boy gave his account—the forest was a dark, menacing place, and it had taken all his wits and determination to negotiate its dangers and come back unharmed. He had sat up sleepless all night under a tree, unsheathed sword in hand.

The Master shook his head slowly. 'You are not ready.' His impassive face betrayed no emotion, not even disappointment.

The boy went back to his dormitory and began to reflect afresh on the mystery that lay behind the Master's words. He must have got it wrong, then. Maybe the forest was a symbol of the territory he would one day inherit. If so, it was not only necessary to survive it but also to know every feature of its topography, to understand it mentally and physically, to establish his power over it. Gathering fresh provisions and declaring to his fellow novitiates that this time he would truly master the forest, he set out again. When he returned after a few days, the Master repeated his question.

'I traversed the whole length and breadth of the forest!' the boy pronounced confidently. 'I know it like the back of my hand! I can draw its full map for you...' He went on excitedly in this vein; his sense of achievement could hardly be contained. But when he had finished, the Master shook his head again.

Another failure! This time, the boy retreated into a shell. He didn't speak a word all day and that night; when the others had all fallen asleep, he silently made his way out of the monastery. In the morning, finding the boy absent, the others grew concerned. Had he set off for home, then, frustrated and defeated? Should they send out word in advance, to the boy's father? Had he returned to the forest, for one last attempt to master it? Perhaps he had journeyed to some other, unknown place, never to return. But the Master was unfazed. Days passed, then weeks and whole months, and slowly, this proud boy who could not fit in became a dim memory.

And then one day, when he was almost forgotten, the boy returned. His clothes were in tatters, hair long and matted, and in his hand, he carried not his sword but a staff hewn from the rough branch of a tree. But this dishevelled appearance belied a quiet glow that was now visible in him. He was taken before the Master, who, never in doubt as to where he had been all this while, merely repeated his earlier question.

The boy spoke without ostentation, but at length, describing how he had allowed his senses to grow accustomed to the forest. Rather than be forever alert to face danger, gradually he schooled himself to calm his mind, to the point where his fears had all been overcome within himself. Knowing that his provisions would soon run out, this time he had taken none, living instead on what the forest had to offer—fruits, nuts and water from the clear spring running through it.

There being no one to talk to, he took to speaking to himself, and when the novelty of that passed, he began to teach himself the art of listening. Birdsong, wind and rain, animal calls and the soft lament of leaves falling as the season turned—not only was he able to distinguish between these sounds, but each one seemed imbued with its own unique emotion and message. They spoke to him. It was only when he felt sure that he was truly one with all these elements in the forest that he decided to return to the monastery.

Now, the Master smiled. The boy was ready to go home.

The Importance of Leadership Training

The takeaway from this Zen story is simple. While true leadership entails a high level of emotional maturity, this quality cannot be imbibed overnight; rather, it must be built gradually and painstakingly over time. It's not an entitlement that a person can lay claim to once he has attained a position of power nor is it about knowing or conquering the forest; rather, it is about being connected and truly becoming one with the elements. Great leaders are inspiring and people want to follow them because such leaders have the ability to touch their hearts and engage with them at a basic emotional level. Seen through this prism, leadership is a function of emotional intelligence.

What does it take to reach this level of maturity? In the terminology of the theory of learning, one is required to make the journey from Conscious Competence to Unconscious Competence. An example will make this clear. Remember the time when you learnt to drive a car or ride a bike. You were picking up this skill while being conscious of every move—pressing the brake, turning a corner, slowing down at the lights, and so on. Over time, this competence became a sort of unconscious, natural proficiency, and the act of driving became effortless without much thought.

The boy in the Zen story was not ready although he survived nights in the forest and knew its topography well; he had not yet reached the level of Unconscious Competence. Likewise, a true leader is one who has gone beyond merely understanding his responsibilities in a theoretical sense, becoming one with the elements that constitute leadership, demonstrating them whenever the need arises. From mechanically performing the task of 'leading' to becoming a true leader is a long journey.

The main crisis in top management today is perhaps not so much the dearth of professionals with the right industry and domain credentials, but a shortage of senior personnel with a high level of emotional enablement. Although with time and perseverance, such skills can be imbibed even later in an individual's life, the benefits of an early schooling in the art of leadership are unbeatable.

Discussions of what constitutes ideal leadership-grooming are neither new nor uncommon. From the time of the ancient Greeks, history abounds in elaborate normative constructs of conduct, ethics and values. And regardless of the extent to which they may have been implemented in reality, for centuries, the study of such philosophical theories was part of the standard education for the youth.

Contrast that with our present-day curricula. Are you likely to be mandated to study treatises of the ancient Greek philosophers for your regular class assignments (unless you're majoring in philosophy)? Quite unlikely! But here's the natural counter-question: If the study of how human beings should live and lead is so essential, how come it no longer forms a part of contemporary mainstream curricula? If it was such an indispensable part of education in times past, why has it dropped off the list since?

The answer, in our opinion, has to do with both expediency and the priorities of our present age. Any syllabus today essentially endeavours to fit in as much 'necessary material' as possible into a given time frame. Education and jobs or the prospect of employment are inextricably linked. Time being the chief constraint, the content of courses is thus prioritized in favour of those subjects that are best deemed to prepare students for today's workplace.

STEM and Its Discontents

In our times, we have witnessed a revolution, whereby increasingly sophisticated technologies have formed a ubiquitous part of our lives.

From mechanization to automation, robotics to artificial intelligence, miniaturization to nanotechnology, software to embedded systems, Internet to the Internet of Things, technology is not just transient but advancing by leaps and bounds. Accordingly, there has been greater focus on those disciplines that aid careers in these fields. In other words, a curriculum based on science, technology, engineering and mathematics (STEM).

The acronym STEM, coined by the US National Science Foundation, was proposed as a new focused approach to education, in response to a market problem faced in the mid- and late '90s. Those were the heydays of the Technology Revolution, with a seemingly endless demand for engineering, science and IT skills in the US economy that far surpassed the number of graduates in these disciplines joining the workforce. Demand for jobs in these fields was greater than supply of skilled manpower, and this demand was expected to remain high! In fact, it was felt that a sustained shortage of these niche competencies would see the US fall behind its economic competitors. This reinforced the urgent need for a STEM-based education system.

And so, this new model came into prominence, to fill the demand for specific skills. As the Technology Revolution spread across the globe, particularly to countries such as India, where it played a major part in fuelling economic prosperity, the STEM-based education also began to take root there. And for quite a while, this system of emphasis on technical or 'hard skills' continued to dominate in many parts of the world, with relatively less focus on what are commonly called 'soft skills'.

However, twenty years on, the picture in the US has changed; this time, though, the realities are far harsher. The notion of a long-term, secure 'STEM job' has been debunked as a myth and even the once glamorous IT sector has lost its former sheen, with giants like IBM forced to back down on their earlier no-retrenchment policy. The outsourcing of jobs on a large scale, particularly in IT, resulted in largely stagnant wage levels in the US. As jobs and associated skills have become increasingly commodified, the individual has been rendered more dispensable, and employer loyalty has diminished.[1]

Demographer Michael S. Teitelbaum, who has studied the data for STEM graduates and corresponding statistics for employment for these skills, has argued that there is scant evidence of the claimed widespread shortages in the US science and engineering workforce. His work reveals that unemployment rates among scientists and engineers have remained higher than in other professions such as physicians, dentists, lawyers and registered nurses.

Teitelbaum's conclusion is telling: 'Far from offering expanding attractive career opportunities, it seems that many, but not all, science and engineering careers are headed in the opposite direction—unstable careers, slow-growing wages and high risk of jobs moving offshore or being filled by temporary workers from abroad.'[2]

Now, turn the lens to India. From the standpoint of the US and other economies that have outsourced jobs over the years, India has been one of the principal beneficiaries. But viewed from an internal standpoint within India, a different side of the picture emerges:

- It is now widely accepted that the 'gold rush' years of the IT industry are behind us; consequently, the demand (even for outsourced jobs) has shifted from traditional programming skills to more niche ones, but the number of such personnel needed is relatively low.
- Being a globalized economy, India isn't insulated from uncertainties in other parts of the world; consequently, recessions in the US and other economies can and do have a downside in the Indian market, including the lowering of demand and the prospect of large-scale retrenchment.
- The schemes centred around skill development and apprenticeship, as well as programmes such as Start-Up India, urgently advocated nationwide by the government, attest to the fact that state-run enterprises as well as corporates aren't able to absorb the numbers graduating from colleges across the country. Thus, there is a need for expertise-building, self-reliance and employment creation at

an individual, micro level to sustain economic growth.
- Rising wages in India and diminishing cost arbitrage opportunities have made matters worse, resulting in even lower demand for traditional programming skills.
- Among Indian engineering graduates, there is still a rush for technology or consulting, where wages are relatively high and careers are perceived to be glamorous, at the expense of careers in other sectors, e.g., scientific research.[3]
- Along with falling demand, there is rising supply with thousands of colleges giving out engineering and science degrees, thereby making the demand–supply gap even larger. This only confirms what we mentioned at the start—the 'gold rush' years of the IT industry are indeed behind us.

The complex mosaic emerging across geographies and economies points towards one conclusion: STEM by itself is no longer the full answer. While expanding an individual's cognitive abilities, it does not prepare him emotionally to adapt to the increasing pace of change. Nor arm him with the abilities to continuously unlearn, relearn and acquire new skills, to influence and motivate self and others, and to continuously deliver value in a workplace requiring higher-order thinking. Any framework claiming to be holistic and comprehensive can no longer ignore the dimension of emotional enablement.

The Power of ESTEEM

As the disparities become evident—between the availability of STEM-skilled resources on the one hand and the demand in the market for those skills on the other—two key questions appear:

- If not STEM, what disciplines in this changing order of things should education embrace?
- While it is accepted that going forward, economic growth will be largely driven by continuous innovation, how would the skills for creativity and innovation be institutionalized and standardized?

There is an ongoing debate between the proponents of STEM and their critics. The champions argue that the principles of STEM can be found in virtually every discipline, that they aren't limited to the subjects of science, engineering, technology or mathematics alone. Rather, technical knowledge and the scientific mindset of inquiry go hand in hand with creativity, leading to innovative ideas across disciplines.[4]

The critics of STEM contend that exposure to the wider discipline of the arts equips a person better for decision-making, creativity and innovation. In their view, it is not deep scholarship but practical application of the arts that sets one up for success. Thus, alternative frameworks such as STEAM and STEMMA have entered the discourse.[5]

Our own position is that there's need for a holistic programme that advances empathy, understanding and creativity, alongside technological savvy. STEM does not necessarily provide answers to the problems of today's world—ignorance, poverty, intolerance and political conflict. Our capacities for ethical decision-making, compassion and creativity must also grow in tandem with our ability to operate sophisticated technology and gadgets. This can be supported by a framework such as ESTEEM, where EE stands for emotional enablement.

ESTEEM can be distinguished from the other frameworks in several aspects as below:

- With STEM and others, there is an advocacy of specific disciplines that, according to their proponents, are suitable for the marketplace, followed by the attempt to retrofit them into an existing model. In ESTEEM, our approach is fundamentally different—the focus is on emotional enablement and the full range of skills it encompasses.
- Therefore, ESTEEM does not champion or prescribe any particular discipline; instead, it underscores the need to explore what disciplines would best work to provide a comprehensive and holistic education to today's youth. Thus, a grounding

in the humanities may end up being a worthy addition in the ESTEEM curricula. As may the discipline of positive psychology or neurosciences.
- STEM, STEAM and other alternatives are all educational models that concentrate on the fitment for today's job market—there is minimal discussion of continued self-development once one enters the workforce. On the other hand, in the ESTEEM framework, this initial preparatory phase is merely the starting point; the emphasis is on how the life-long journey of each individual is a process of making them emotionally enabled.
- ESTEEM does not profess to be a superior framework; it is a platform for a model of longer-term success and well-being. Our gauge is that the study of a given discipline under an ESTEEM-based model may in fact make a person more employable. We believe that emotional enablement allows a person to cope better with the vagaries of an increasingly uncertain job market.
- Emotional enablement prepares an individual for professional accomplishments over a longer time frame. Routine and repetitive tasks across industries are increasingly getting automated, and many jobs that previously involved manual operating are now dying out. ESTEEM provides a more viable framework for success in the jobs of the future.

Emotional Intelligence Revisited

In our parlance, we consider emotional enablement to be the process or journey to the Unconscious Competence zone of emotional intelligence, where it becomes second nature. And here, it'd be useful to sketch out what emotional intelligence entails. The term EQ or emotional quotient (as compared to IQ or intelligence quotient) is used interchangeably with emotional intelligence. During the course of writing this book, we asked various people what EQ means to them and we learnt that EQ means different things to different people. Which is perhaps not so surprising, given that the concept itself is still relatively new, live and evolving.

Interest in EQ gained vogue in the '90s, the principal researcher in this field being Daniel Goleman. His bestselling book *Emotional Intelligence: Why It Can Matter More than IQ*, published in 1995, remains a seminal work in the field even today.[6] In this work, Goleman introduced the concept of emotional intelligence, which according to him accounts for 80 per cent of success in life. Over the past two decades, he has continued his research, publishing several more books and papers on the subject, in the process further crystallizing his framework. In Goleman's model, EQ can be viewed in terms of two pairs of complementary dimensions—one being Self & Others and the other being Knowledge & Management.

The diagram below represents these in the form of four quadrants:

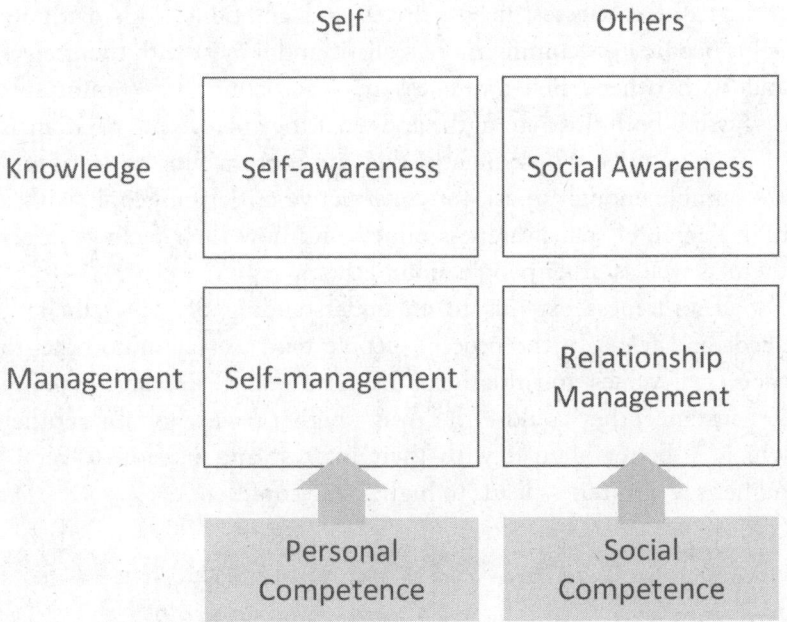

Figure 5.1: Four quadrants of emotional intelligence

These key skills of emotional intelligence pair up under two main competencies—personal competence and social competence. Personal competence is about (a) knowledge of ourselves (self-awareness) and (b) the ability to manage ourselves (self-management skills). In comparison, social competence is made up of (a) our knowledge of others' feelings and emotions (social awareness) and (b) the ability to manage relationships with others (relationship management skills).

The four skills taken together make up emotional intelligence. Self-awareness and self-management are more about us and our internal selves. On the other hand, social awareness and relationship management are more about how we are with other people.

Self-awareness

Self-awareness means having a deep understanding of one's strengths, weaknesses, needs, drives and emotions. This attribute helps people in becoming more realistic and honest with themselves and with others. Self-awareness makes them more comfortable discussing both their strengths and what they perceive as their areas of improvement. Consequently, they are more willing to learn and are humble enough to ask for constructive criticism. People with a high degree of self-awareness understand how their feelings affect them as well as other people around them.

Self-awareness extends to an understanding of values, beliefs, needs and fears. In the process, people tend to stay more 'true' to their own values and this helps in more ethical decision-making. For instance, they could turn down a higher paying job for another which is better aligned with their interest and passion. Overall, higher self-awareness leads to higher self-confidence.

Self-management

It is one thing to be conscious of our emotions and to be in touch with them, but managing them is quite another. Sometimes, we find this challenging as our emotions can be quite overwhelming. And again, where does one draw the line—between 'managing emotions' and 'going with the flow'? While one's ability to withstand emotional storms is often praised as a virtue, a life devoid of emotion and passion would be boring.

And this is where the challenge lies—the human brain is designed in a way that often we have little control over when we will be swept away by emotions or what those emotions will be. The saving grace is that we do have some control over how long they last. Self-management is thus like an ongoing inner conversation, freeing us from being prisoners of our feelings. People with higher self-management skills feel bad moods and emotional impulses just as everyone else, but they are able to control them better and sometimes even channelize them in positive ways. Among other things, it enables them to better cope with ambiguity and change and also be able to say no to impulses that can end up harming them.[7]

Social Awareness

The more self-aware we are, the more skilled we become at recognizing the feelings of others. Empathy, defined as the ability to sense others' emotions and 'put oneself in the other's shoes', lies at the core of social awareness. Those who can read others' feelings are certainly better adjusted and sensitive, if not more well-liked. Empathy is particularly important today as a key leadership trait, given the demanding and disrupting effects of multiple teams, globalization, the hunt for better talent and the constantly rising standards of professional efficiency.

An empathetic leader is able to sense any dissonance in the viewpoints of all members of the team and across teams, without getting influenced by any particular individual or group. Globalization raises the challenge of cross-cultural dialogue, presenting higher chances of misunderstanding. As the war to secure the best talent intensifies, leaders with empathy are able to develop and retain good people through coaching and mentoring. Instinctively, they sense the best way to give feedback (and very importantly, when to give it!); they know when to push and when to hold back, thereby demonstrating empathy in action.[8]

Relationship Management

In a way, advanced social skills are a cumulative effect of the other dimensions of EQ. People become effective in managing relationships when they can understand and control their own emotions and also empathize with the feelings of others. This combination makes them expert persuaders and team players, and good mentors. You know you have perfected the art of leading people when you as well as the people you lead see these interactions not as instructions or orders, but as being part of a symbiotic relationship.

ESTEEM—Key States of Being

Goleman and other researchers have established an analytical framework that allows us to study the various tenets of EQ and their interrelationships with each other. Building on this, we have identified four core traits or 'states of being', mastery of which would allow us to operate at the Unconscious Competence level of EQ, to enable a better day-to-day experience of life, on both personal and professional fronts. These four key states—Being Mindful, Being Realistic, Being Reflective and Being Empathetic—are outlined below, and are discussed in depth in the subsequent chapters.

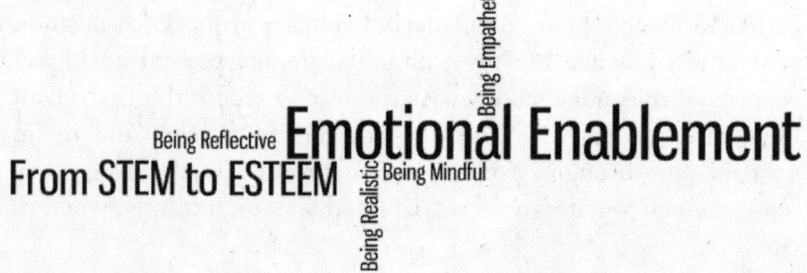

Being Mindful

In today's always-online, fast-paced world, we feel compelled to multitask, but our minds struggle to maintain focus. We log into conference calls during our morning walks, respond to emails on our phones over breakfast and plan the morning's meeting while driving to work. And then, during the actual meeting, we find it hard to concentrate, find ourselves thinking instead of, say, the imminent tax returns for that fiscal.

The result is that we are never in the moment, and we don't realize that this in turn causes havoc in our lives. We flit between activities without paying attention to our thoughts and feelings, almost as if we are automatons. This prevents us from stepping back to look at the big picture, prioritizing our work, maintaining focus, keeping to deadlines and being more productive overall. It also hampers our ability to connect emotionally with others. Ultimately, we lose touch with ourselves and end up leading shallow lives.

Being mindful is all about being in the moment, becoming more aware of what we're feeling, more thoughtful about our actions and behaviours and more attentive to the impact we create on others. It's about this 'presence', which is such an important building block of emotional enablement. Mindfulness can be seen as the opposite of mindlessness. When we mindlessly do something, we rely on automatic routines and often let the past decide the future.

However, being on autopilot often makes us respond instantly to a stimulus. Since we may not be able to control the environment which creates the stimulus, we become victims of our surroundings. By being mindful on the other hand, we are able to press the Pause button between the stimulus and response. This can be immensely liberating because we are now able take control of our actions and are not merely driven by our surroundings.

Being Realistic

Diwali, Christmas and New Year are joyful times for all. We think back on the twelve months gone by and many of us decide to bring in fresh changes to our lives. With all good intent, we make New Year resolutions—to make new friends, drop weight, join a gym, spend more time with family, and so on. But once we get back to work, the pressure builds up quickly. Weeks speed past, and before we even realize it, all those nice resolutions become wishful thinking, a thing of the past, not likely to be taken up seriously.

Leaders and managers often find themselves in situations where they take on unrealistic deliverables and deadlines for their teams. While they couch the challenge as 'stretch goal' to be achieved, the personnel reporting to them view it almost as an impossibility, engendering panic and low morale in its wake. And all this because the decision-making in the first place has not been realistic.

Several factors contribute to this phenomenon. First, there is what social psychologists call the 'Overconfidence Bias' or 'Illusory Superiority'. This feeling, causing people to overestimate their own abilities, is more common than we realize. Try this simple test. Next time you are with a group of friends, ask them the question: 'How many of you are better-than-average drivers?' for a self-assessment score. In a typical unbiased sample, statistically speaking, you'd expect to have 50 per cent of your friends raising their hands. Compare this to the actual number who do so!

Secondly, the challenge of having to do more in less time. Our workdays are hectic and packed anyway, so that any additional commitment that we take on inevitably threatens to stress us out. But on top of this, new projects are sometimes brought in without properly closing out previous ones. Everyone starts feeling the pressure and, without operative means of renewal, this leads to chronic stress. Even joining the company wellness programme ends up feeling like yet another task to be achieved within an ever-shrinking time frame.

The way to declutter our lives is to take on only those things which are essential, and let go certain things or habits that have either outlived their purpose or were perhaps not that useful in the first place. We all know that to a large extent, it is possible to achieve a sense of balance, through effective delegation and planning. Yet, when it comes down to it, many of us falter on both these fronts.

Being realistic does not imply that we never aim high. We may indeed set our goals high, but at the same time need to find a mechanism of being able to reach them through several steps of continuous improvement and progress. Contrary to earlier popular understanding, our mental and emotional faculties are known to develop throughout our adult lives. Hence, as we come out of our comfort zones and reach for our stretch zones, over time, those activities become part of our new comfort zone. And what was earlier in the panic zone now falls within our stretch zone.

Being Reflective

Being reflective helps in taking a very objective, dispassionate look at our actions and behaviours, associated emotions and feelings, and overall state of mind. While this may sound somewhat narcissistic on the face of it, the ability to be reflective and the practice of it is one of the best means of improving ourselves continuously, of making course corrections and striving to achieve our goals.

For any learning to be real, it must be manifested in our actions and the way we conduct ourselves. And this in turn requires us to continually toggle between action and reflection. In today's world, given the paucity of time and with so much to accomplish, we are often in the action mode with little time left for reflection. While action is critical for us to keep moving towards our goals and become more efficient in our skills and jobs, reflection helps us in being more effective, i.e., by doing the right things, and not just doing things right.

Let's say you try to prepare a new dish and go with a recipe you found on the Internet, but unfortunately, it does not turn out too well. Would you use the same recipe the second time around? Chances are you would either adjust the recipe or find a new and hopefully better one. When the outcome is clear for us to see (the taste of the dish), we reflect on it and make adjustments. But often, the outcomes are not clearly understood right away (e.g., telling off a team member) or the outcome is clear to someone else but not to us (not sanctioning leave for a team member). This makes it all the more important to reflect on those actions to enable us to make good decisions going forward.

A clear majority of us suffer from the proverbial knowing-doing gap, i.e., we know (most often) what we we're supposed to do but often end up not doing them. (Remember those New Year resolutions!) For example, you may decide that spending time with your family is an important value for you. But you need to reflect not just on that value but also on whether you are living up to that value, i.e., how often are you *actually* spending time with your family? We need to keep some time aside to ask ourselves some key questions periodically, particularly if they seem to be uncomfortable. Am I using my time wisely? Am I living true to myself? Am I taking care of my health? Am I taking my job, colleagues, juniors or perhaps even my boss for granted? Am I achieving the goals I have set for myself? And so on.

It is important for the act of reflection to focus on positives, not just negatives. This creates positive emotions, which are directly linked to our emotional well-being and happiness, and convinces us that we are making progress. Research on motivation reveals that the most important factor in boosting a person's motivation is the feeling that they've made progress in doing meaningful work.

Being Empathetic

This key strength, which is the innate connection to the thoughts and feelings of others, is an essential component of emotional intelligence. It helps build mutual trust, deeper bonds and eventually, better relationships with family members, friends and colleagues at work. Essentially, empathy is the ability to identify and understand another's situation, feelings, needs, concerns and motives. This means 'putting yourself in the other person's shoes' or 'seeing things through someone else's eyes'.

Empathy is about both thinking and feeling. We need to use our reasoning ability to understand what the other person could be thinking and feeling and truly making an effort to stop and think for a moment about the other person's perspective and begin to understand where they are coming from. But we need to be careful not to overthink and start forming opinions which is a natural tendency for most of us. Rather, we need to stay clear of judgement and just understand their perspective, and recognize *their* perspective of what they believe to be *their* truth.

As humans, we have an inherent ability to do this. Neuroscientists have discovered a type of neuron called mirror neurons which are involved in empathy; just as there are neurons in our brain which fire when we perform an action, there are mirror neurons which fire when we're looking at somebody else performing the same action. It is as though this neuron adopts the other person's point of view.

Unfortunately, while we have the intrinsic ability to feel for others, today's fast-paced life coupled with constant media coverage of violence and negativity has an adverse numbing effect on us. Consequently, we are becoming hard-nosed and hardened and, ultimately, dehumanized. The pressing need here is for us to start *feeling* once again.

A good means of understanding another person's perspective is to develop our listening skills. We often listen to respond rather than understand. People with high empathy will be fully focused on the other person when they are listening and, in some cases, even mirror the emotion and body language of the other person, thereby building trust. Empathy has huge implications in the business world. Be it as leaders or junior team members, we need empathy and we need to care for people realistically.

6

Being Mindful: Alive and in the Moment

Land's End—Avik's Story

This was in 2012, when I was based in the UK. At the end of a particularly gruelling work phase, my wife and I took a few days off. Slogging back-to-back through weekends had left me totally exhausted and badly in need of rejuvenation. So, we planned a leisurely tour of Cornwall, finishing off with a trip to Land's End, which promised a spectacular view of the Atlantic. The bus from Penzance dropped us off at the stop, arranging to pick us up on the way back, after sunset.

For some reason, there were very few tourists around and as the bus drew away, we were left in the midst of this ethereally stunning scenery. But thoughts about a sales proposal I'd been working on kept distracting me. As Shikha walked on ahead, I felt compelled to make that phone call, although I was on holiday. And over the next ten minutes, even with this fantastic sight before me, it seemed as if some screen separated me from it, inscribed with deadlines, deliverables and worry.

Finally, I was at her side. 'I am certainly going to come back here!' I exclaimed, gazing out at the waters.

Shikha looked at me, surprised. 'Why're you talking about coming back? You *are* already here!'

It took me a moment to figure out what she really meant. After all, I'd just spontaneously said the first thing that came to me;

there wasn't anything to read into. Then the true import of her words sank in and I gazed at the view anew, with a fresh pair of eyes.

All the brochures, travel magazines and postcards with their marketing superlatives could not have done justice to it. Before us, ragged granite boulders rose and plunged dramatically into the waves of the Atlantic. We took one of the walking paths that trailed along the cliff line, the wind in our faces. Sun-rimmed clouds hovered low over the horizon, shifting constantly, forming and un-forming shapes that had no name.

As we looked on, the vast vault of the sky appeared to tilt, and the sun returned from cloud cover to sheathe the unbroken stretch of water all around in lush, burnished gold. Immersed in this endless moment, we just looked at the view, speechless; not once did the thought of taking out a camera cross our mind.

And I realized how my work-related deliberations had cut me off from my surroundings. In making that phone call, I had jumped ahead in time to the duties of the week ahead. No wonder then that I couldn't appreciate the view, and in my mind, this trip to Land's End was already a thing of the past, even though I was still very much right there! Clearly, I had given the sense of living in the moment, without judgement or distraction, a miss, allowing in its place a kind of numbness that prevented me from enjoying the full beauty of that setting.

What Causes This Numbness?

When we're not living in the moment, our lives are consumed by tasks, activities, projects, deadlines and constant, unrelenting pressure. So, more often than not, we miss out on the myriad 'little things' in our daily lives—celebrating someone's birthday at work, the completion of a milestone or commending a team member who put in an all-nighter. And this blasé lack of acknowledgement of the little accomplishments that do matter has adverse implications for motivation at the workplace.

This numbness that makes us miss out on the little things ultimately puts us out of touch with our feelings. It reduces our emotional intelligence, since we are unable to connect with our inner selves and do not feel an emotional connection with others. Various factors contribute to this let us explore them.

Quite apart from our own non-stop thoughts, the sheer quantum of data we deal with in today's Digital Age is mind-boggling. At a fair estimate, we are bombarded with 34GB of information every day—enough to fill a laptop in a fortnight! We have so much to understand, to think about, to process, and we need to take numerous decisions, all based on our deliberations. When presented with more information, our natural reaction is to try to speed up even more, to match the ever-increasing influx of data. We are left with little time to pause, reflect and feel.

Regrettably, being 'extremely busy' has become the model for a successful life, typically handed down from those in the workplace we are supposed to emulate. Many of our readers may be familiar with such a personage in their workplaces. A very senior person at the workplace turns up for meetings looking drained, and announces to everyone that he hasn't slept for the last three days, as he has been taking care of an escalation! Subtext: *If I can work so hard and for so long, why can't you?*

Thus, we stay up late to read through pending mails. We tweet, press the Like button on Facebook and make our own updates; we stay connected with our network on LinkedIn, but all of this takes its toll. Not only do we keep working longer hours, we allow less time for renewal of energies, even though we feel the need for it.

And this inability to make time for rejuvenation in turn takes a toll on our ability to feel both for ourselves and for others, which is absolutely essential for any kind of emotional stability. The busier we are, the more important we seem to ourselves. The need for recovery is seen as a weakness and we feel guilty about admitting the need for it.

Along with working longer hours, we try to accomplish more in a given period of time. We multitask. In a milieu where being in touch with our emotions is regarded as a liability, almost with some suspicion, multitasking is seen as an asset and a virtue, especially in the workplace. Someone who can respond to emails while eating lunch or take an urgent call during a team meeting is commended no end and touted as a role model for the rest of the team. But does multitasking really enhance productivity, as is generally presumed?

Try this exercise. Take your pen and on a sheet of paper, in the first line on top, write the following. (Replace Vineet with your own name.) And record how long this task took you to complete.

```
M  y  n  a  m  e  i  s  V  i   n   e   e   t
1  2  3  4  5  6  7  8  9  10  11  12  13  14
```

Below that, write numbers for each of the alphabets above. That is 1 below M, 2 below y, 3 below n and so on. Now, repeat this activity, but with one significant difference. Instead of writing out the whole sentence on a single line first and then the numbers in another single line below it, now write 'M' and then 1 below it, then write 'y' and then 2 below it, write 'n' and 3 below it, and so on, till you complete the sentence. Time this activity.

Unless you're an outlier, we expect that the second activity (i.e., writing the sentence and the numbers in vertical, rather than linear, fashion) will take you around 20–30 per cent longer to complete, if not more. Now, ask yourself this—which of these approaches made you more comfortable? Also, in which one did the quality of the writing turn out better? You will almost certainly agree that the first approach is faster, more comfortable to execute and produces a better quality. This exercise is a good analogy of what multitasking does to us. When we split a finite amount of time allotted to us to doing too many incongruous activities, our focus and concentration levels suffer, and with it, our effectiveness and productivity.

Every now and then, we try to break away from this vicious circle by taking a vacation. But even leisure feels busy and we find ourselves in a constant 'doing' mode. Think of the clichéd question you hear among jet-set travellers—'how many countries did you visit in your last European vacation?' Chances are you made sure that all the Lonely Planet recommendations were ticked off your list! How many times have you felt tired instead of rejuvenated, after you are back from a break?

Living in Autopilot

Do you remember being very conscious of brushing your teeth this morning? No, you just did it automatically, right? Or can you recall in detail the drive or commute from your home to your workplace this morning? It's probably a blur; you were thinking of the day ahead. The explanation behind this is pretty simple: Our brain has a lot to process, and whenever it finds something repetitive, it tends to store the 'algorithm' as a sort of program. That way, it reduces the cognitive load. So, every time we brush our teeth, the brain runs a 'brush teeth' program with the same actions playing out every time. The program runs in our subconscious mind.

When it comes to driving, some of it is subconscious (e.g., turning the ignition, putting on the seat belt, changing gears, etc.) but not all of it, especially given the state of traffic (and drivers!) on Indian roads. However, the automatic program running in the background helps us to open up our conscious brain for other activities not related to the job at hand. It enables us to think and do other things.

Isn't it also the case that just like that morning drive to work, the whole day sometimes passes by quickly, in a blur, and before you realize it, you're already on your way home? At such times, it's likely that you won't be able to recall the details of the things you did all day. If this sounds familiar, you're not alone. In fact, it has been found that most people spend almost 47 per cent of their waking hours thinking about something other than what they're doing. In other words, many of us operate on autopilot.[1]

Neurologically speaking, 100 billion nerve cells or neurons within our brain are interacting with other neurons through connections called synapses, in an unimaginably fast and dynamic network.

When we do something repeatedly, the neurons in our brains fire together. As we repeat these actions, they eventually wire together, making the process an unconscious habit.

However, this phenomenon of automaticity which helps us by reducing our cognitive load also brings its own challenges. We can spend our whole lives in the 'doing' mode. With everything happening automatically, we lack a connection with the true essence of things around us, so that we scarcely notice them and yet have this lingering feeling that we are missing out on life. Which in turn leads to a perpetual sense of dissatisfaction.

On your way to work, suppose you're driving past a beautiful children's park, a patch of refreshing green amidst all the city concrete, and you see some children playing. If you're on autopilot, you're already thinking of all the issues at work, what needs to be done, how to tackle the next project, and so on and so forth. If so, you will miss the peaceful sight of children playing and the accompanying music of laughter and innocence. If you do notice it, however, (i.e., you are able to come out of your automatic behaviour mode), you may be amazed at the beauty of it. This simple connection with the sense of sight and sound is an example of being in the moment. The state of mind changes by shifting the focus of your attention to the present moment. You're no longer on autopilot, but in the present moment.[2]

The mass of information hurtling towards us from all sides daily is unavoidable, but trying to catch and process it all is a big mistake. On the contrary, the faster those waves come, the more deliberately we should try to navigate them, to avoid getting tossed around. Never before has it been so important to filter out selectively and prioritize what's truly important.

For true emotional enablement, we need to break the cycle of doing more and more and feeling less and less. We have to develop the ability to come out of autopilot when required so that we aren't doing and thinking different things. We should reconnect with our feelings, to focus and renew ourselves, to live in the moment rather than living in the past or worrying about the future. In other words, we need to be mindful.

What Is Mindfulness?

In today's frenetically paced world, we seem to be always on the move. Even when we are sedentary, our minds are constantly in motion, fraught with a ceaseless stream of thoughts and ideas. Our daily schedules have almost 'programmed' us to the extent that if we're not doing something all the time, it makes us uneasy. And if we see others sitting quietly by themselves, the sense of idling away time becomes pronounced. 'Don't just sit there, do something!' This is what we'll likely say to that person. We all have a natural bias for action.

Which is why the notion of 'sitting and doing nothing' runs completely contrary to our present-day thinking. But mindfulness is essentially that—'non-doing' instead of doing, the cessation of conscious thought that keeps driving us around, and the beginnings, however simple, of a meditative state of mind. Mindfulness is about training our brain 'to be' with what's there instead of needing 'to do' something about it. And for many of us who live in our heads, it can be difficult to implement this in our daily lives. For nearly every waking moment, we are so used to doing something either with our bodies or our minds that breaking away from what has become second nature can be knotty for us, especially as we start this journey.

During Nelson Mandela's hugely publicized visit to France to visit President Francois Mitterrand, the press asked Mr Mandela what he'd like to do the most. The answer came as a surprise to many. 'What I want to do the most is to just sit down and do nothing.'[3]

But how exactly does one go about doing that, you may wonder. Not only are our minds on continuous hyperactive mode, they have a natural tendency not to follow instructions. Try this out. Read the following slowly, taking each word in.

STOP THINKING OF THE BLUE ELEPHANT

Now, surely all imaginings about a blue elephant would have been furthest from your mind up to the point when you actually read these words above. But now, if you close your eyes and try to make your mind go blank, how tough it is erasing any notion of that absurd creature! As humans, we can't help but think. It's as natural to us as breathing and often, it happens far more frequently! In fact, scientists estimate that human beings can have up to 60,000 thoughts in the span of a single day! A scary thought in itself.

Mindfulness, however, is not an attempt to shut down our thoughts. Rather, it's attaining a state where we become dispassionate observers of our own thoughts and actions, of all that's happening around us. A popularly used metaphor is that of a waterfall. Imagine you are standing somewhere behind a waterfall, which is flowing down in front of you. You can see and hear the water but it's not pouring directly on you. You are observing it, yet not immersed in it. Consequently, you are in no danger of getting swept away by the water and going downstream with it.[4]

This waterfall is the incessant flow of our thoughts, feelings and emotions. Normally, we are right in the thick of it, carried along by its great force and turbulence. Overwhelmed by this constant surge of emotions, we let them take us where, in a more mindful state, we'd never have wished to go in the first place. Being buffeted by the current of the waterfall, we are unable to find inner peace.

However, if we manage to step out of it, we will find that we're able to observe our thoughts, acknowledging them from a distance, without judgement or bias. And this helps us to 'let it be', when the situation calls for it, so that *we* can then decide what to do with that thought or emotion instead of *it* being in control of us. Being mindful doesn't take away the problems of our lives; however, it allows us to respond rather than react to our lives' problems.[5]

The Emotional Brain

Mindfulness helps us even more during times of stress. Stress brings to the surface negative emotions and in this condition, unconscious thinking is usually negative thinking. When we are not in the present moment, our mind is in the past or future. It often takes the form of reliving something that has already happened over and over again—something we regret or miss or a loss of opportunity that continues to haunt us. It is as if our mind is obsessed with the push of the past ('I just can't forgive what he did') and the pull of the future ('I can't wait to quit and give my manager a piece of my mind') like a monkey swinging from tree to tree. This 'Monkey Mind' takes you out of the moment and out of what is best for your life.[6] It's only when we turn our attention to the present and focus mindfully on what we're doing at this moment that we are able to break away from regrets and worries and truly live in the moment.

It's worthwhile understanding how our brains react to stressful situations or the reasons why negative emotions exist in the first place. The most primitive component of our brain, which hasn't evolved in over 100 million years, is the reptilian brain, whose main function is to protect us from threats. This is the part that is always on, scanning all stimuli for threats. This reptilian brain is also in charge of our vital functions, such as our heartbeat and maintaining body temperature. It is the 'me' brain and it is only concerned with the present, not the past, not the future.

As living beings evolved into social animals, living in groups and caring for young ones, the 'we' brain evolved, concerned with not only the present but the past as well. Emotions and memory thus came to be associated with this new mammalian brain, also known as the limbic system or 'emotional brain'. This section of the brain, though a more recent evolution, is still fifty million years old.

Back in prehistoric times when we were constantly under fear of attack from wild animals and other sources of danger, stress was a survival mechanism. Emotions helped to prepare our body to act in emergency situations. Faced with a threat, the emotional brain would invoke what psychologists call a 'fight or flight' response. If the brain decided on 'fight', it would invoke anger and blood flow to our hands would increase so that we could more easily grab a weapon or strike with it. For a 'flight' response, it would invoke 'fear'; the heart would pump furiously to increase blood pressure; glucose would be sent to the muscles as fuel injection; stress hormones such as cortisol are released in the blood, all so that we could start running really fast to get us out of danger.

These physiological reactions were essential for survival in those early times. For the limbic system or the emotional brain, acting on impulse was appropriate for the harsh conditions our prehistoric ancestors lived in. Then, about 2.5 million years ago, man developed a highly intelligent wrinkly 'neocortex', also known as the 'thinking brain', which enabled abilities such as complex thought, consciousness, language and imagination, differentiating man from other species. This part of the brain can visualize the future, and its workings are not just limited to the present or past.

While our thinking brain is in charge most of the time, the emotional brain takes over when it comes to emergencies. If a lion enters the room you are in right now, your brain would trigger a flight response and you would be running to save your life. You wouldn't stop to think—OK, what should I do now? Or—is this lion going to eat me? No way, you'd just run! Thinking (or overthinking) in such a situation would have you end up as the lion's meal, within minutes. Faster than the neocortex, a part of the brain called amygdala reacts to threatening scenes before rational thinking occurs.

Interestingly, in the way that the human brain has developed, this prehistoric, reptilian and emotional brain has not been stripped away. In emergencies, the emotional brain takes over or 'hijacks' our thinking brain in what is called an 'amygdala hijack'. This phenomenon is named after the amygdala, which plays a primary role in the processing of memory and emotional reactions.

Today, fortunately, we are not faced with the physical dangers which our ancestors faced during prehistoric times. However, our brain is not able to differentiate between a physical and social threat. This sometimes causes us to freak out under stressful (but by no means life-threatening) situations and behave in ways we come to regret later.

Thus, we could suddenly snap at our partner or boss, or react badly to a situation, or fall prey to road rage, and only much later, wonder—

what was I thinking? The truth is—we weren't! The amygdala hijack ensured that our thinking had momentarily stopped.

Even when the situation is not so grave as to trigger a full-scale hijack, a threat from stress results in similar but relatively less intensive responses such as stress chemicals being released in our bloodstream, palms sweating, a butterflies-in-the-stomach feeling, impeding clear thinking on our part. And here too, albeit in diminished intensity, the fight-or-flight instinct takes over. Thus, a person might get aggressive in getting his point across (fight) during a disagreement in a meeting or just decide to keep quiet and avoid any sort of confrontation (flight), even though he may have a point of view that differs from those of the others.

How Mindfulness Counters Fight or Flight

Mindfulness helps in countering the fight-or-flight stress response and even a full-blown amygdala hijack. Mindfulness—being conscious of what is happening to our body and deep breathing—helps us press the Pause button between a stimulus and a response. It is for this simple reason that we are told to take deep breaths when we are angry.

In acknowledging that emotion, we're telling ourselves—I realize that I am feeling very angry now—and in the process, we return to the thinking brain, from the emotional brain. We are able to create a distance between the thought and the thinker, the feeling and the person feeling it (feeler), and between the impulse and the action, allowing us to press the Pause button.

Mindfulness and Meditation

On one level, mindfulness is really a form of meditation, known as mindful meditation. During mindful meditation, we observe and acknowledge our thoughts and emotions and at the same time, we continually bring our awareness back to the here and now. This is the act of 're-centering' through breathing, as we consciously focus on our breathing. This re-centering is essential because we *will* get carried away by our emotions or thoughts and then we *will* tend to judge them. Even as you read these sentences, are you truly mindful? Or have your thoughts wandered off elsewhere?

Re-centering trains the brain to increase concentration and focus. In the waterfall metaphor of mindfulness, re-centering through breathing gives us an anchor so that we don't get swept away downstream with the water. With practice, we can become more aware of our breath and begin to consciously pay attention to it.

The concept of mindfulness is thousands of years old, tracing its origins to the teachings of the Buddha. In traditional Buddhist philosophy, there is the concept of what in Pali is termed 'Sati', which is the seventh element of the noble Eight-Fold Path and is therefore one of the attributes leading to enlightenment. While literally meaning 'memory', a more apt translation is 'mindfulness'.[7]

Mindfulness is the state of constant vigilance in which one has a clear, unbiased comprehension of everything taking place around oneself. Far deeper than a mere theoretical concept, it is a Buddhist practice that various sects over time have honed to a high state of evolution. Mindfulness is linked to Vipassanā meditation, which has now gained popularity worldwide. The key to mastery is in the practice of it, in making it an integral part of one's daily life, maintaining as much as possible a calm awareness of one's body, mind, thoughts and emotions, pacifying the mind and strengthening one's power of concentration.

In the 1970s, Jon Kabat-Zinn, a molecular biologist from New England and a long-time meditator in the Zen Buddhist tradition, believed that many people who could otherwise benefit from meditation were being turned off by allusions to reincarnation or other religious associations that clung to it. So, he devised a new and pleasing definition of mindfulness, one that now makes no mention of enlightenment: 'The awareness that arises through paying attention on purpose in the present moment, and non-judgementally.'[8]

Scientists are discovering that many traits (e.g., temper, compassion) and abilities (e.g., talent, intelligence) that we have always considered fixed or innate are actually acquired skills. They are not inborn virtues; rather, they should be viewed more like muscles, which can strengthen with exercise. Mindfulness meditation is also a mental exercise and it needs to be built into a habit.

Unfortunately, there are some common myths and misconceptions associated with meditation. People often turn to meditation as a form of escape from all the pressures of life. But that is not what meditation is about. It is not about shutting off but about observing thoughts. There is also a fair amount of scepticism. Part of us wants to practise meditation, to achieve some swift tangible improvements in our lives, yet are cynical about believing they will really take place. There is also the proverbial knowing-doing gap, which means we are not consistent in our habits. If we told you to start meditating right away, as you're reading this page, and showed you a few steps, you may think:

> *This is a bit too spiritual or religious for me*
> *Not sure if I'm meant for this*
> *It's just a lot of hype*
> *It's difficult to scientifically test its real benefits*
> *It's a pseudoscience—not the real deal*

So Why Bother? Suman's Take

I can readily relate to these questions, since I had *exactly* the same thoughts when I first approached meditation. Being a totally analytical person with a deep respect for science, I was sceptical about mindfulness and any tangible benefits that would accrue from meditation. As an engineer, I found myself constantly asking—*where is the empirical evidence*? But as I started to do some research, I grew more convinced of its scientific underpinnings. Slowly, I began to experience some positive results for myself, which reinforced my belief.

In the wellness workshops which are part of my firm's offerings, we devote at least fifteen minutes to a meditation session. We ask participants two questions before starting the session:

How many of you meditate?
How many of you meditate daily?

Interestingly, about 20–40 per cent of participants respond in the affirmative to the first question. But the moment we add 'daily', the number drops significantly.

People typically tend to think of meditation as 'doing' and not 'being', and take it up for various reasons—to relax, to feel something special or to reduce stress or pain. All good intentions notwithstanding, there is always the expectation of results, quick ones, just because we happen to be meditating. We expect that special, other-worldly experience, and if we don't see something happening pretty quickly, we get disheartened and start doubting whether we are 'doing it right', or whether the whole thing works at all!

Benefits of Meditation

There has been a lot of interest globally, in the great Indian traditions and philosophies, particularly related to yoga and meditation, and some of the greatest icons, whether from industry or the arts, have sworn by them. It is well-known, for instance, that Steve Jobs used mindfulness meditation to reduce his stress, gain more clarity, and enhance his creativity. 'If you just sit and observe, you will see how restless your mind is,' Jobs told his biographer, Walter Isaacson. 'If you try to calm it, it only makes it worse, but over time it does calm, and when it does, there's room to hear more subtle things; that's when your intuition starts to blossom and you start to see things more clearly and be in the present more. Your mind just slows down, and you see a tremendous expanse in the moment. You see so much more than you could see before. It's a discipline; you have to practise it.'

In the first half of the twentieth century, the German Nobel laureate Hermann Hesse used meditation as a central theme running through many of his greatest works, including *The Glass Bead Game*, *The Journey to the East* and *Siddhartha*. In *The Glass Bead Game*, the protagonist Joseph Knecht, while undergoing a personal crisis as a student, approaches an experienced Master for guidance. And the Master, recounting his own student-day experiences, tells him: 'The fact is, Joseph, that the more we demand of ourselves, or the more our task at any given time demands of us, the more dependent we are on meditation as a wellspring of energy.'[9]

Literary masterpieces apart, there is a plethora of material available on meditation, from spiritual treatises and books on esoteric rituals to DIY manuals. But among the most lucid are the writings and teachings of the acclaimed Indian philosopher J. Krishnamurti. Eschewing the rigours and austerity traditionally associated with meditative practices, he demystifies it and discusses it at a level that makes it widely accessible, without diluting its principles and values. In his words: 'When you learn about yourself, watch yourself, watch the way you walk, how you eat, what you say, the gossip, the hate, the jealousy—if you are aware of all that in yourself, without any choice, that is part of meditation. So, meditation can take place when you are sitting in a bus or walking in the woods full of light and shadows, or listening to the singing of birds or looking at the face of your wife or child.'[10]

The benefits of meditation are many—reduction of stress; easing of symptoms of depression, pain, anxiety disorders; improved immune function; reduced blood pressure; enhanced cognitive function; enhanced focus; and improved quality of life. These benefits are being scientifically validated through techniques such as fMRI, and today, there's enough evidence to substantiate what the great sages have been saying for millennia.

It has been found that mindfulness prevents burnout and boosts compassion among physicians, which may improve the doctor–patient relationship. And some hospitals have actually started bringing mindfulness into their facilities. Meditation has been integrated into the medical profession by what is known as Mindfulness-based Stress Reduction (MBSR), developed by Kabat-Zinn.

For students, it can boost focus, attention and memory, lower stress levels and improve sleep quality, and some studies have even found mindfulness training to improve test scores. It is helping to promote resiliency and well-being among soldiers and to relieve symptoms of Post-traumatic Stress Disorder (PTSD). In the present day, meditation is proving to be immensely helpful to people from varied walks of life ranging from students to doctors to soldiers.

Brain Activity during Meditation

In recent years, there have been significant advances in our understanding of how the human brain functions. Through techniques such as functional MRI (fMRI), scientists can now study activities in different parts of the brain and draw inferences about how the brain behaves under different situations and stimuli. This research nevertheless sheds fascinating new light on certain aspects, for example, on how meditation affects brain activity.

The long-term results of meditation, as evinced from researches in neuroscience, are no less fascinating. Studies show that labelling negative emotions reduces the intensity of activity in the amygdala. The scans show that after an eight-week course of mindfulness practice, the brain's fight-or-flight centre, the amygdala, appears to shrink. And as that happens, the pre-frontal cortex (PFC)—associated with higher-order brain functions—becomes thicker. This means that the change in the amygdala is not responding to the change in the environment; rather, it's representing the change in people's reaction or relationship to their environment.

Meditation is shown to reduce levels of cortisol, a hormone related to stress. When cortisol levels drop, the mind grows calmer and gains the stability to become more focused. This ability has profound implications for leadership. At a time when a team is facing severe crisis and team members are under high stress, a leader who is calm and can think clearly can get the team out of the situation, with minimal pain or hardship experienced in the process. A leader should also be in touch with team members emotionally, understand their thinking, anticipate and address threats that might invoke fight-or-flight reactions in them.

Meditation rewires our neuro-circuits, pruning away the least used connections and strengthening the ones we exercise most. It also increases the volume and density of the hippocampus, crucial for memory. Thus, Buddhist monks who have practised it for several years have robust connections between different regions of their brain, which facilitates synchronized communication. They also develop a particularly wrinkly cortex used for the most sophisticated mental activities, such as abstract thought and introspection. Such people have scored higher on tests on attention and working memory. Regarding visual attention, some fifty- or sixty-year-olds can even outperform twenty-year-olds.[11]

The unambiguously calming effect of meditation can also be seen through a brain EEG or Electroencephalogram. Similar to what an ECG is for a heart, an EEG provides evidence of spontaneous activity in the brain, and its findings in meditators are nothing short of remarkable. The brain emits different types of waves depending on our mental and physical state. The different types of EEG waves are depicted in the diagram below.

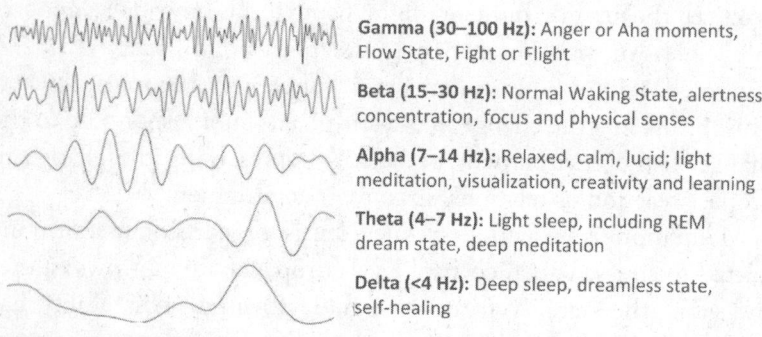

Figure 6.1: EEG brainwaves

Our most common EEG state is Beta, where waves are at a frequency of 15–30Hz. This is our normal waking state, associated with alertness, concentration and focus on our tasks. The Alpha state is a relaxed and calm state which we experience when we wake up and when we are about to fall asleep. The Theta and Delta states are associated with light and deep sleep respectively.

Meditators show an Alpha state during light meditation and a Theta state during deep meditation. In other words, during deep meditation, the brain activity is similar to that of light sleep and even during light meditation, the brain experiences a relaxed and calm state typically associated with creativity and learning. Such is the calming effect of meditation!

Pit Stops for a Mindful Day

Formula One is exciting to watch. The speeds are incredible, often upwards of 300kmph. What it takes to be a winner is much more than the performance of the car—the skills of the driver not just in manoeuvring at high speeds but also his techniques of stopping for fuel and maintenance. Those brief stops are called pit stops.

Just as an ultra-high performance machine needs to recharge itself momentarily, think of your pauses during the day as pit stops—not time-wasting but essential for renewal. Since you too are geared for high performance at full speed, those pit stops become essential. Just as pit stops are total stops and not merely slowing down, your mindfulness pit stops need to be total 'non-doing' and should not be about action at all.

Below are some simple techniques that you can incorporate into a typical workday. The idea is to get started slowly, deliberately, on the journey of mindfulness. We can say from experience that this regime, if practised daily and over a period of time, will begin to reconnect you with the experience of living in the here and now, despite all the distractions our busy lives pose for us.[12]

6:30 a.m.—Waking Up. Before starting any high-performance sport like sprinting or swimming, athletes prepare themselves by being completely still, listening for the gunshot to signal the start. Similarly, start your day with an inner stillness so that you can give your best to the day ahead.

Once the alarm goes off, resist the temptation to check mails and messages on your phone or of getting into immediate action. Instead, spend a few minutes in your bed, paying close attention to your breathing as it moves in and out of the body. As thoughts about the day ahead keep coming, acknowledge them, then let go and return to focusing on your breath.

Studies show that our body releases the most stress hormones right after waking up, as thinking of the day ahead triggers the brain's fight-or-flight response and releases cortisol into the bloodstream. Hence, the need for stillness before we start. If possible, devote more time in the morning for renewal and rejuvenation. You can meditate, do yoga, write a gratitude journal or whatever else that helps you to be mindful.

8:00 a.m.—The Drive to Work. Since driving triggers automatic behaviour in our brain, use this part of your daily routine to help you practise conscious thinking and improve your mindfulness—feeling your hands on the steering wheel, the gear change, the seat belt against your body, the foot on the pedal. A mindful commute will help you become more focused, relaxed and effective once you get to your destination.

9:00 a.m.—Work Desk. At your work desk, use the few moments that your computer takes to boot up to practise some mindful breathing. Make a conscious effort to soak in the feeling of sitting in your chair, take in the sights and sounds in your immediate environment.

9:30 a.m.—Meetings. In a meeting, there are various thoughts in your head about the rest of the day ahead but try to stay focused and listen to what each speaker has to say. Unless absolutely essential, avoid taking your laptop to the meeting, and put your phone on mute to avoid distractions.

10:30 a.m.—Multitasking. Back at your desk, resist the urge to multitask. Identify the one or two key tasks that you need to address on priority, rather than dividing time between mails, phone calls, social media and breaks.

11:30 a.m.—Pit Stops. Set a phone reminder telling you to take a pit stop. At this time, with so much going on, there'll be numerous thoughts going on in your mind as you close your eyes. Again, don't try to shut down your thoughts. Instead, just notice, acknowledge, feel your chest rise and fall and refocus on your breath.

1:00 p.m.—Over lunch, practise mindfulness by savouring the colours, textures and flavours of the food. Thereafter, if you go for a short stroll, practise mindful walking, being aware of each step and of your breath.

1:30 p.m.—Presentations. Putting the final touches on an important presentation, you reach out to a colleague for some inputs you need for that meeting. He gives you the bad news that his part is not ready yet. Suddenly, you feel your stomach clench and your heartbeat shoot up as you realize that you won't be ready for the upcoming meeting. Take a deep breath and feel the emotions going through your body. As you tell yourself—*I am feeling angry (or panicky) right now*—you consciously re-engage the executive control centres of your brain and thereby avoid that amygdala hijack!

2:30 p.m.—You call your boss, asking if you could reschedule your presentation, apprehensive of her reaction. She tells you that it's too late to reschedule as there are other key players in that meeting and you need to make that presentation at the scheduled time. As you make your way there, take a mindful breath before walking in. In those few seconds, draw full attention to your breath, thereby resetting your mind and body.

There is a scientific explanation as to why even one mindful breath can be calming. Breaths taken mindfully are slow and deep and this stimulates the vagus nerve (one of the cranial nerves), activating the parasympathetic nervous system. Doing so lowers your stress, reduces your heart rate and blood pressure, and calms you down.

4:00 p.m.—The meeting could've been better. You faced a few embarrassing questions about the gaps in your presentation in spite of your best efforts. You settle back at your desk and compose an email, summarizing the discussion, action items and concerns raised during the meeting. Before you hit that Send button, take a deep breath, reflect on the key message you are trying to send across and remember there are human beings receiving your message, not computers.

Over time, you will be able to train your brain to associate simple daily events such as sending mails, answering the phone or touching a door handle before entering the meeting room as cues to practise mindful breathing. Collecting yourself with a deep breath during such touchpoints will help you to respond rather than to react to situations.

5:00 p.m.—Time for another pit stop. Take a break from 'doing' to practise the state of 'being'. Is your body relaxed or tense? Are you feeling anxious, restless, bored or tired? Acknowledge and re-centre, using your breath to anchor yourself in the present moment.

7:00 p.m.—Heading Home. As you prepare to set off for home, take a few moments again to practise mindful breathing during the time it takes for the computer to close all its applications and shut down.

9:00 p.m.—Family Dinner. As you sit down for dinner with family, be mindful of the plate in front of you—feel the aroma of rising steam from good, hot food. Food not only serves as fuel for the body but also nourishes the mind and uplifts the spirit.

11:00 p.m.—As you lie down, take a few deep breaths and feel good that you have fully lived every moment of the day!

On a normal day, with just these few interventions, you will be well on your way to start being in the present and enjoying every moment of it. On other days, when you find yourself stuck in a massive traffic jam or having to sit through a lengthy meeting which isn't of interest to you, look at those instances not as time wasted but as excellent opportunities for practising mindfulness.

A Quiet Revolution

Time magazine called the growing popularity of meditation a revolution, devoting an exclusive edition to this subject: 'The

Mindful Revolution'. In January 2015, during the World Economic Forum in Davos, Switzerland, Kabat-Zinn led executives and 1 percenters in a mindfulness meditation meant to promote general well-being. Many in pinstripes and conference lanyards also took time away from panels on Bitcoin and cyber security to communally breathe, and to attend a packed session called 'The Human Brain: Deconstructing Mindfulness'.[13]

Slowly but surely, meditation is entering the corporate space. Several organizations across industries such as Google, Target, General Mills, Apple, McKinsey & Co., Taj Hotels, Deutsche Bank, Procter & Gamble, AstraZeneca and Mindtree have all introduced meditation sessions in the workplace. According to Mark Coleman, who teaches meditation at Google Search Inside Yourself Leadership Institute training: 'Mindfulness is the foundation of emotional intelligence.' At the training, hosted by Coleman and Search Inside Yourself CEO Marc Lesser, participants undergo attention and mindfulness training exercises designed to build emotional intelligence. 'Mindfulness, in the context we're teaching it here, is the same as self-awareness,' says Coleman. 'We're teaching self-awareness. We can develop the capacity to be more aware, to be more attentive, to be more mindful.' At the crux of the programme's philosophy is the idea that attention and self-awareness set the stage for leadership success.[14]

Without mindfulness, our brains tend to miss what's happening in the here and now. We miss the facial reactions of other team members; we see threats instead of opportunities and miss chances to praise and recognize team members before jumping into problems and solutions. In other words, we lack emotional intelligence. Practising meditation is a powerful way to get back in touch with our own and others' emotions.

How Mindful Are You?

There is a vast literature on the subject of mindfulness. From the earliest philosophical underpinnings of the Buddha's sermons to meditation tips, workbooks, questionnaires and psychometric considerations for scoring, it's a long list.[15]

The questionnaire below presents situations you are likely to experience on a daily basis, but which helps you gauge the level of your own mindfulness. There are no trick questions. As you work your way through it, you'll no doubt have a sense of what the 'best possible' responses are likely to be, for each given situation. However, it's important that you answer according to what really reflects your experience rather than what you think the correct response should be. Record the scores and retain a copy of this assessment. From 'Never True' to 'Always True', the scores range sequentially from 1 to 5. Over time, as you continue to work on your mindfulness and you return to take the test again, you'll most likely find that your scores have improved.

Sr #	Situation	Never True	Rarely True	Sometimes True	Often True	Always True
1	When I'm walking, I deliberately notice the sensations of my body moving.					
2	When I have distressing thoughts or images, I am able to simply notice them without reacting.					
3	I notice visual elements in art or nature, such as colours, shapes, textures, or patterns of light and shadow.					
4	Even when I am terribly upset, I can find a way to put it into words.					

5	I do not make judgements about whether my impulses are good or bad.					
6	I find it natural to stay focused on what is happening in the present.					
7	I notice how foods and drinks affect my thoughts, bodily sensations and emotions.					
8	In difficult situations, I can pause without immediately reacting.					
9	I tend to get into the 'flow' at work without getting distracted.					
10	I watch my feelings without getting overwhelmed by them.					

If your scores are between **10** and **23**, then you tend to operate more on 'autopilot'. Read through the examples and case studies in the book, try to apply the principles of mindfulness in your daily routine.

If your scores are between **24** and **37**, it indicates that you have the workings of mindfulness embedded in your personality.

If your scores are between **38** and **50**, then you have already evolved as a mindful individual. Continue to apply mindfulness on a daily basis to enjoy a more fulfilling life.

7

Being Realistic: Compassion, Motivation and Purpose

Being Your Own Best Friend

It is said that we're our worst critics and, on the whole, this is probably true. Think back on the last time you failed to achieve a goal—whether an academic one, or landing that coveted post or promotion at the office or the desired level of raise, or knocking an extra inch off the love handle—there'd have been that inevitable let-down when you missed the mark.

Now ask yourself if what you wanted to accomplish was a well-defined goal in the first place—or simply a wish. Did you have a clear plan in mind? Did you make a plan, develop it into a routine and monitor progress regularly? Were you confident and optimistic all through? In other words, were you being realistic in the way you set about achieving this goal?

'Being realistic'. It's a phrase we often use, and yet we miss out on its true import. Being realistic enables us to become our own best friend. We often cut some flak for our dearest friends, treating them with kindness, affection and compassion, overlooking mistakes, occasional hurts and disappointments, without lowering our estimates of them. If we did that, we'd fast run out of friends and well-wishers!

However, very rarely do we treat ourselves with a similar level of compassion. When we fail to achieve any of our goals or milestones, frustration, anger or, at times, even a sense of self-loathing takes over. We dub what has transpired as a failure. We are constantly under pressure from an inner judge who is relentless and unforgiving. And so introspection in the aftermath of a 'failure' quickly turns into severe self-criticism, and the ensuing torrent of negative emotions leaves us exhausted and ready to give up. Being realistic allows us to build up reserves of self-compassion, affording us a better chance at achieving the milestones we set ourselves, because now we are able to enjoy the journey too, not just the outcome.

The ability to be practical and realistic is extremely important in order to maintain any kind of effective relationship. Things can go very wrong if, implicitly or explicitly, we set wrong expectations and then get disappointed when things don't turn out the way we expect. In our lives today, we often find that there is more and more to do and less and less time to do it all in. Those of you who work with a to-do list, on both personal and professional fronts, will relate immediately to this. You may find that, over a period of time, your to-do list has only grown larger. This means that more items are being added to the list on a daily basis than you're able to tick off.

Now take a step back and review the items that have featured this past week in your list, or variant thereof, such as calendar appointments, alerts and reminders on your phone. Chances are you'll find that at least a few of these items are self-inflicted, particularly as it relates to the workplace. Instead of taking on only the key tasks for the day each morning and successfully bringing them to completion by close of business, you take on several things.

But in doing this, you run the risk of being dejected, not seeing visible progress on the to-do list, not completing tasks on time, not being able to prioritize between them, and not achieving the level of quality that we or others would like to see. Sure, some of these items may've been thrust upon us, wherein we have no choice but to execute. But more often than not, we do have a choice and we willingly take on new tasks.

Self-assessment: Too Much or Too Little?

At some level, we all believe that we are rational in our thinking and decision-making. And being realistic is integral to any kind of rational thinking and decision-making process. Why then do we still face such difficulty, sometimes without even being aware of it, when it comes to being realistic?

One reason is that most of us tend to overestimate our qualities and abilities. Social psychologists call this phenomenon 'Overconfidence Bias' or 'Illusory Superiority'. It is more common than most of us realize. It is similar to the 'it can't happen to me' syndrome, with which we are familiar each time we hear about someone else's failure. For instance, when we hear of someone else losing a job or a loved one, suffering from a critical illness such as a stroke or cancer, or getting robbed, something within us tells us that this is a rare event and somehow, we are not susceptible to such situations.[1]

A study conducted some years ago asked a group of 700 engineers from two large Silicon Valley companies to assess their own performance relative to their peers. The results were startling. Nearly 40 per cent felt they were in the top 5 per cent. About 92 per cent felt they were in the top quarter. Only one lone individual felt his performance was below average.[2]

Overconfidence Bias, when people compare themselves with others, shows up in different aspects of life, including academic performance in exams or overall intelligence, in work environment aspects such as talent and job performance, as well as in social settings, in terms of popularity and confidence. This in turn nudges us to take on more than we can possibly achieve, and also hinders our ability to delegate some of our work to others. Since we feel that no one else can do the job with the same level of dedication and perfection as we do, we hesitate to distribute work tasks and hold onto them ourselves. Left unchecked, the same leader who was once seen as a high achiever when promoted to a senior level is suddenly a single point of failure for the team.

Besides the Overconfidence Bias, there could be other psychological and behavioural issues at play, which push us to take on more. Taking on more makes us feel more important and notches up our self-worth. We give the impression that we are capable of handling more workload than others. When we're unable to deliver, we blame our circumstances, thereby keeping our self-worth intact. Also, saying no is sometimes viewed as a weakness. Peer pressure may also be a factor, or a sense of what management expects of you. Your superiors at the workplace may tend to show tacit disapproval, when you start saying no.

Whatever be the reason, taking on more and then not being able to keep the commitments has serious consequences. We rationalize our actions by our intent (which is good) but others judge us by our actions and behaviour. In the process, we do not come across as trustworthy and tend to lose their trust. In our own minds, inability to meet our personal goals results in lowered levels of confidence and perseverance.

Motivation and Willpower

A good place to start is to focus on setting realistic goals and targets. In our constant striving for self-improvement, we set ourselves a list of lofty goals. For instance, your goals may include a morning walk regime, losing weight, spending more time with family, taking more vacations or taking out more 'me time', reading more articles and posts in the areas of your interest, writing a blog, strengthening relationships with your manager(s) and improving your communication skills. There's a good likelihood that a majority of those goals have been there on your list for a few years now. If this is the case, you're not an exception! For a majority of us, there is a big gap between our wishes, goals and targets and our ability to execute them.

Getting things done requires both motivation and willpower. Motivation is the sense of 'I want to do this' sustained over a period of time. Willpower is the conviction behind 'I will get this done' sustained through the point where your goal is met. If you're motivated to improve your fitness coefficient (true for both the authors here!), you will still need sufficient willpower to be able to execute the plan. On the other hand, even if you have the willpower to work on your fitness, you may quickly lose the motivation to continue, especially if your initial efforts are not rewarded by any discernible improvements. Therefore, for any real progress, we need to strengthen both our motivation and willpower levels simultaneously.

Being realistic in our goals helps us experience the small wins on a day-to-day basis. And this has huge implications for our motivation, in that it can make a big difference in the ways we feel and act. Researchers have called this the Progress Principle. Being able to see real progress triggers positive emotions like satisfaction, happiness and joy. It leads to a sense of accomplishment and self-worth, in turn fuelling motivation, commitment and engagement.[3]

There is an explanation for the Progress Principle in neuroscience and it involves dopamine, the 'pleasure' hormone that is linked to motivation. It has been found that anything the brain perceives as a reward, even the expectation of a positive event, generates dopamine. Every small win gives you a splash of dopamine, and a series of such small wins guarantees a steady supply of dopamine, sustaining high motivation levels.

Willpower, it has been interestingly discovered, is a finite resource. You get a certain amount of willpower on any given day, and once you've exhausted that amount, you'll find it difficult taking on other tasks. This probably explains why we're unable to work on all our different goals simultaneously and follow through on each of them.

One of the best ways to strengthen willpower is to turn it into a habit. Willpower may be a limited resource, one that's extremely hard to replenish. However, when the activity becomes a habit, we do it almost without thinking.

According to Angela Duckworth, a researcher from the University of Pennsylvania conducting research on students: 'The best way to strengthen willpower and give students a leg up is to make it into a habit. Sometimes, it looks like people with great self-control aren't working hard—but that's because they've made it automatic ... Their willpower occurs without their having to think about it.'[4]

Research shows that the habits of highly successful people allow them to consistently behave in ways that breed success. They depend more on habit than sheer drive and ambition to keep them focused on their goals. Everything from eating well to fitness to responsible spending and task completion requires habits that make such behaviours part of our daily lives.

But building habits takes time. Till then, one needs to fall back on sheer willpower. All this is changing the way scientists look at self-mastery. Instead of trying to take on multiple tasks, the focus is now on allowing oneself to handle just a few and building habits around them till they become automatic. Only then is it time to take on more goals and employ a similar approach to habit formation. In other words, an incremental, 'baby steps' approach instead of a dramatic 'big bang' one.

The good news is that even if we pick up just one or two key actions or tasks and are able to successfully transform them into habits, these 'keystone habits' trigger a process that starts a chain reaction and transforms everything. In the process, other existing patterns can be altered, calibrated, or even discarded and replaced by others, over time.[5] Exercise, to pick an example, is a keystone habit. Once people get into the habit of exercising, they also start to change other, unrelated patterns in their lives, often unknowingly. For instance, they start eating better, become more energetic and productive, feel less stress and show more patience with colleagues and family members. Overall, it triggers widespread change.

So how do you go about creating a habit? For one, the activity needs to be done continuously for several days for it to become automatic behaviour. In a study published in the *European Journal of Social Psychology*, Phillippa Lally, a health psychology researcher at University College London, and her team decided to find out just how long it actually takes to form a habit.[6] The study examined the habits of ninety-six people over twelve weeks. Each person chose one new habit for the twelve weeks and reported each day on whether or not they carried out the behaviour and how automatic the behaviour felt. From 'drinking a bottle of water with lunch' to 'running for fifteen minutes before dinner', a number of habits were chosen. The conclusion of the study was that on average, it takes more than two months (~sixty-six days) before a new behaviour becomes automatic, i.e., a habit.

Vision—2020

If we feel inundated with our chores and challenges on the personal front, the problem is only compounded at work. Somehow, the truism 'less is more' seems to be at odds with the workplace. There are always more goals and more stretch targets and more things to accomplish, never less. As employees, we're constantly trying to manage our ever-increasing workload. As leaders, we are forever setting larger and bigger goals for our organization, our teams and constituent team members.

Particularly interesting is the amount of time, effort and money that organizations invest in coming up with targets, and the gusto with which they then market it internally, to employees. It is as if these goals themselves will motivate the workforce. Companies love to set very ambitious and nice-sounding goals—'We will be a USD 20 billion company by 2020'. This, by the way, is a recent goal set by Infosys, one of the India's top IT companies. During the announcement, they termed the four-year targets 'aggressive and ambitious'. Sometime after this announcement, there was a press report, saying that some senior leaders already felt this target was more *aspirational*—a euphemistic way of saying 'not really achievable'. [7]

The question we need to ask is: What impact do targets such as these have on employees in the organization? Are such ambitious goals realistic or merely aspirational? Are they creating motivation and willpower for its employees or having the opposite effect? Here again, motivation primarily stems from the Progress Principle and the importance of feeling that one is making strides towards achieving it.

There is one essential difference though, when it comes to workplace targets. While a target of losing five kilos in three months is a good personal goal and lends itself well to the Progress Principle, a stretch sales goal of 20 per cent for the year does not have a similar impact as a team goal. To be able to motivate people across departments and levels, the goal needs to be more than just a number; it needs to have meaning and purpose that is shared by the people who execute on the ground and achieve it.

This is a daunting task. In fact, there is so much scepticism, it often finds its way into *Dilbert* and other cartoons. A *New Yorker* cartoon shows a worker supporting himself with one hand against a wall and the other clutching his chest. 'Really, I'm fine,' he says to his concerned colleagues, 'It was just a fleeting sense of purpose—I'm sure it will pass.'

"*Really, I'm fine. It was just a fleeting sense of purpose—I'm sure it will pass.*"

Figure 7.1

The cartoon makes a keen observation—that for many people, work so often feels soulless. It comes as no surprise that only a third of US employees are fully engaged in their work as per a recent Gallup survey.[8] The corresponding number for India is even lower.

Now, we all know that corporate vision and mission statements are meant to define the organizations, to outline the reasons they exist. Here's a simple test. Stop reading right now and write down your organization's vision. If you don't seem to remember, you are in good company—70 per cent of people can't. Most people either don't know their organization's vision, or don't understand it, or feel so disconnected from it that they can't explain how it relates to their day job.

Yet, most organizations do have a vision statement, often a pretty elaborate one. If you look at the vision statements of some of the world's leading organizations, they go beyond financial targets and delve into values and behaviours. But unfortunately, they often look and sound similar, using clichéd jargon. For example: *'By creating value for our customers, we create value for our shareholders. We use our expertise to create products and services of superior quality, safety and environmental care for demanding customers in selected segments...'* Do you feel in any way inspired now?

An example of a great vision statement is the one that President John F. Kennedy uttered, in his address to Congress in 1961: 'I believe that this nation should commit itself to achieving the goal, before the decade is out, of landing a man on the Moon and returning him safely to Earth.' NASA took up this vision, and Project Apollo came into being, eventually turning it into reality, in 1969. Making this happen required the most sudden burst of technological creativity and the largest commitment of resources ($24 billion) ever made by any nation in peacetime. At its peak, Apollo employed 4,00,000 people, supported by over 20,000 industrial firms and universities.[9]

Such a short and simple vision statement had a very powerful impact. It galvanized a whole nation into action. Kennedy's goal was accomplished on the *Apollo 11* mission when astronauts Neil Armstrong and Buzz Aldrin landed their Lunar Module on 20

July 1969, and walked on lunar surface. What made the vision so powerful was that it appealed to the emotions of all those committed to the goal. A stretch target—but realistic! And amazingly simple to understand for everyone in the organization and beyond.

The Need for SMART Goals

All organizations do not carry such lofty goals. And they don't need to. While the work that employees carry out may be relatively mundane, a realistic vision infused with meaning may still motivate them. There's this story of a mason who looked weary and dull when asked what he was doing. He responded: 'I am laying bricks.' Another mason looked excited, when asked the same question and while doing the same activity. The second man shot back: 'I am building a cathedral.' It is this mental picture of a desired vision or end-state (cathedral) that acts as a powerful motivator.

Some organizations have been able to craft mission statements that are simple to understand and motivate both externally (customers) and internally (employees). For example, take Google's vision: 'Organize the world's information and make it universally accessible and useful.' Split this statement into two parts—the organizing part of it, and even to an extent making it accessible requires a highly evolved level of efficiency (IQ), but the making information universally useful part of it is essentially to do with EQ. One cannot make anything about people universally useful unless one is totally focused on them, their emotions, needs and aspirations.

Combining a company's ethos with clearly defined numbers can also be very motivating. Take PepsiCo, which, with a basic consumable as its product, nevertheless came up with a goal imbued with a universal sense of purpose. Its CEO, Indra Nooyi, has combined mission with metrics as part of the 'Performance with Purpose' plan.

Here is a clear example of an ambitious, hard-hitting and yet very tangible goal: 'By 2025, at least two-thirds of PepsiCo's beverage portfolio will have 100 calories (or less) from added sugar; in high-risk water areas, 100 per cent of the water used in manufacturing will be replenished; the company will invest $100 million in initiatives that benefit 12.5 million women and girls globally.' There is a comprehensive discussion in the plan, on how the company is making a difference across products, people and planet.[10]

Part of the reason goals such as these are easy to relate to is because they involve the SMART (Specific, Measurable, Assignable, Realistic, Time-related) principle. Analyse this principle with regard to the goal that Kennedy set. In its intention, the vision was quite Specific, nothing vague about it at all. It was Measurable in that the goal was articulated in very tangible terms. Even though the statement didn't identify people or departments, it was obvious that a massive number of resources across a range of skills and capabilities would be required, and in that sense, it was Assignable. Although it may have sounded dream-like at the time of its utterance, history proved that this stretch target was in fact Realistic. And of course, it was Time-related, because the goal was to be achieved before the '60s got over.

So, whether you are a business leader trying to craft a mission statement for your organization or a manager trying to motivate your team around a stated company goal or vision, it's really useful to build a SMART goal that goes beyond financial numbers, something that people can feel or visualize and which appeals to their emotions.

Cutting down or 'de-scoping', a challenging task in the corporate world, is another means of being realistic. Companies often take their leadership teams for retreats or 'off-sites', to brainstorm ideas and strategy. What is also common is that most people complain that the output of those off-sites are not followed through enough for making real change in their respective organizations. The problem is usually one of focus. When there are fifteen 'must-do' items identified from the off-site, it becomes impossible to channelize any company's resources in order to achieve all of them.

Apple is considered to be one of the most innovative companies in the world, and part of this hallowed status was thanks to the laser focus that Steve Jobs had brought to the company. And we can learn from how Jobs used to run off-sites. He would take his 'top 100' people on a retreat each year. On the last day, he would stand in front of a whiteboard and ask, 'What are the ten things we should be doing next?' After much deliberation, the group would come up with ten items. At which point, Jobs would then ask the group to confirm the ranking of these items, slash the bottom seven, and announce: 'We can only do three.'[11]

In his own words: 'Deciding what not to do is as important as deciding what to do.' While this may seem overly simplistic, having the ability to focus requires tremendous courage, conviction and discipline. But sticking to it can reap huge benefits, as companies such as Apple have witnessed. Being focused and realistic is critical to motivating employees, bringing a sense of purpose, harnessing the willpower of team members, and then putting it to good use. But whether it is an individual, a team or an organization, it is critical that we focus on the right things that bring us satisfaction and success. So where *does* one focus?

Knowing Your Signature Strengths

The ability to recognize our own strengths and limitations, without any bias, is the start of our journey to becoming more realistic. This awareness by itself can be powerful, as it helps us negate our Overconfidence Bias. It also sets us on the path of learning; knowing we aren't exactly perfect allows us to leverage others' strengths. But even this awareness can be elusive.

What would you say are your key strengths? When faced with this question in a job interview, many people struggle to come up with concrete, well thought-out points. They respond with weak statements such as 'I am hard-working' or 'I am a team player'. We often go through life with no keen awareness of our real talents and aptitudes and other people may have a better idea than we do ourselves. Try this exercise: Ask three of your close friends to send you a list of your strengths. You may be surprised by what you learn. This is because your friends have the 'clarity of distance', which you don't.

Lack of understanding of strengths—our own and those of others—can have several implications. For one, it becomes hard for us to find our vision or true calling. When we truly enjoy what we do, work ceases to feel like work. We get into what is known as a state of 'flow' in positive psychology, a state in which a person is fully immersed in a feeling of energized focus, complete involvement and enjoyment while doing the activity.[12]

Mihály Csíkszentmihályi, a psychologist noted for his study of creativity and happiness, introduced the concept of 'flow'. He and his team were fascinated by artists who would essentially get lost in their work. Artists, especially painters, got so immersed in their work that they would disregard their need for food, water and even sleep.

At the workplace, the main challenge is not one of identifying the strengths of individuals, but the ability and willingness of management to make use of them. Organizations remain inefficient in leveraging the strengths of its people. Managers typically expect others to excel at performing whatever role is assigned to them, with the tendency to tag the individual, based on just a few selective tasks. So, when a team member does not 'perform' in such a paradigm, the default reaction is to consider removing him from the team or project. Or worse.

In Gallup's well-known employee engagement Q12 survey, involving 1.7 million employees across 100+ countries, one of the questions posed was: 'At work, do I have the opportunity to do what I do best every day?' Shockingly, only 20 per cent of the respondents felt their strengths were in play every day. It also indicated that the longer an employee stays with an organization, the less likely he is to strongly agree that he is playing to his strengths.[13]

As a leader, how should one go about leveraging the strengths of his team members, to get optimum output? An emotionally mature approach would be to assume that each person in the team has some strengths, some tasks that he is naturally good at. So instead of simply removing a team member, one should explore roles that leverage that person's 'signature strengths', and which could completely turn around his performance. If a team member is great at accounting but not so competent at administrative functions, he can be encouraged to work on his areas of strength to take him to the next level. Research has shown that people who build on their signature strengths tend to be happier, perform better at work, be more engaged, and to show higher levels of self-esteem than those deprived of such an opportunity.

This concept of 'signature strengths' stems from Martin Seligman, an American psychologist, educator and author. In his view, signature strengths are these half-dozen or so activities, mental or physical, that feel so good to do that it's almost as if one were made for them. These are the skills one learns quickly, yearns to do, and which energize rather than exhaust one. Giving full rein to these strengths would therefore be a more productive and personally rewarding approach, than pointing to an inventory of one's weaknesses.[14]

Right from a young age, we are expected to learn many subjects, but the focus is always on those where we lag. And this fundamental attitude carries through to the workplace, as we begin our careers. Our managers tell us where we lack skills and create performance-development plans based on those gaps. The emphasis, inevitably, is about fixing what's wrong, not commending what's right.

For a leader, the ability to focus on the vital few over the trivial is critical, as it leaves room for renewal and rejuvenation. There would still be occasional stretch goals, but only to the extent that the team remains motivated, not stretching them to the point where they get exhausted and demotivated. The latter would only result in perpetuating a slave-driving culture in the organization. The leader can also course-correct and is thus able to leverage individual team members' unique strengths and qualities. Aware that not all team members are high performers, when one of them is found wanting, the leader coaches him, pools in help from others in the team and recalibrates his plan, to get him back on track. Asking himself 'What is the person good at?' instead of 'Is the person good?' allows the leader to take a more compassionate view of the person and the situation, thereby building the entire team's morale.

The Three-box Solution

With the rapidly changing nature of business environment, organizations strive to balance the present and the future, albeit with great difficulty. In India, blue-chip companies such as Remington Rand and Metal Box got wiped out because they failed to foresee and adjust to rapid external changes—the personal computer made the typewriter redundant and tetrapacks replaced metal boxes. Globally, things are no different, and the tumbling fortunes of Nokia and Blackberry attest to this.

One main reason why organizations struggle in this regard is the inability to let go of the past. Dr Vijay Govindarajan, author and fellow at Harvard Business School, explains this using what he calls the 'Three-box Solution'.[15]

As the diagram below shows, Box 1 is about managing the present (exploit) and Box 3 is about creating the future (explore). But there is an important component—Box 2—which is to selectively forget the past and is by far the most difficult of all the three boxes to accomplish.

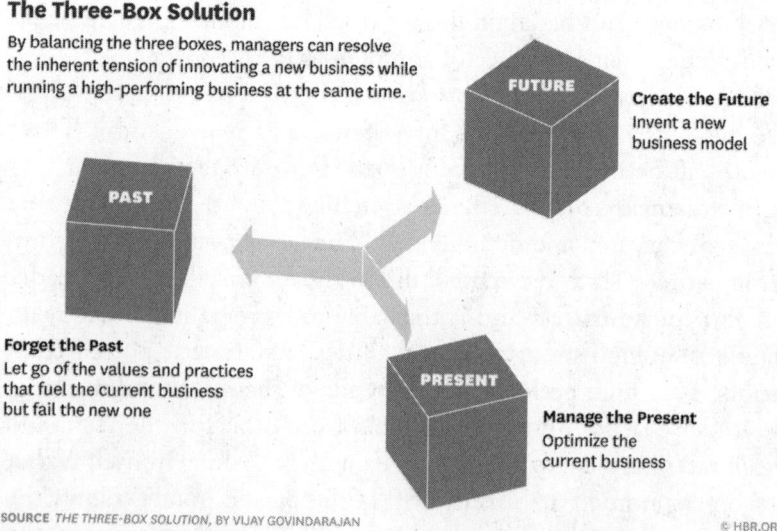

Figure 7.2

Not addressing Box 2 results in an overload on the organization, as more initiatives are brought in when employees are already reeling under pressure. More projects are spawned off when no earlier projects are actively killed to make space for new ones. Old policies and procedures continue even when they hold little relevance in the new environment.

A company can rise to the challenge of disruption by including in its strategy the component of exploit vs explore. Trying to exploit its current strengths, product portfolio and market share helps boost the bottom line and enhance profits. But as these are relatively short-term, the organization also looks beyond this to explore, innovate and bring new products and services designed for the future.

This trade-off and balance between exploit vs explore may also be seen outside the workplace, in our own lives as individuals. We try to exploit our current strengths, network and environment to reap the benefits of what we have. But not addressing Box 2, not being able to forget the past or trying something new becomes a hurdle in the path of reinventing ourselves.

Nelson Mandela grew up as an angry man in South Africa, as he fought against injustice and apartheid. The regime branded him as a state enemy, and he was kept incarcerated for as long as twenty-seven years. A natural fallout of such long confinement would be more anger, bitterness and hatred. But Mr Mandela decided to selectively forget the past in the larger interest of his nation. After coming out of prison, he worked on the fruitful, healing elements in Box 3 to create South Africa's future by reconciliation with the same people who'd been his persecutors.

Interestingly, the Three-box Solution may be said to be derived from a Hindu construct termed Trimurti (three forms), which is the trinity of supreme divinity in Hinduism, in which the aspects of creation, preservation and destruction are personified as a triad of gods. According to this notion, creation–preservation–destruction is a continuous cycle without a beginning or an end. Brahma is the creator, Vishnu the preserver, and Shiva is the destroyer.

Like Vishnu, an organization needs to preserve its existing core; like Brahma, it must create a bright new future; like Shiva, it must also proactively destroy unwanted vestiges of the past to pave the way for the future. So, whether you are trying to bring in personal changes or to transform your team, division or organization, ask yourself—do I have a destroyer inside me and/or my team?

Together with letting go of the past, we need to be good at saying no to new requests and distractions. For most of us, saying no doesn't come naturally. It's a characteristic that's deeply ingrained in our Indian culture. We feel terrible disappointing a friend, guilty about turning down the boss and anxious denying a client's request. We want to be seen not as a 'no' person but a 'yes' person, a team player.

While the intent may be good, taking on too many assignments leaves us stressed. Drawing on our empathy and social skills, we can say no with less chance of offending the other person. But saying no is important to remaining realistic for both our individual success and our organization's success.

In general, people are intrinsically motivated and they don't join organizations thinking they will somehow get by with minimal effort and engagement. Instead, people join organizations with positivity and hope, truly wanting to make a difference. However, their efforts face resistance, criticism, and after a few setbacks, they lose hope and figure out how to adjust and manage in the system as it is.

They continue to face challenges, which have an adverse impact on motivation levels and also chip away at people's confidence. At some point, they start believing that the challenges are insurmountable, that it is futile to push ahead. Therefore, a key ingredient for success is having high levels of self-confidence. Only those who are self-confident can empower others and not feel threatened by their success. That also helps in creating an atmosphere of trust and learning from each other rather than one based on fear.

Jack Welch, the legendary ex-chairman of GE, pegged self-confidence as one of the most important leadership traits. He felt that self-confidence was the antidote to insecurity, which lies at the root of very many ills in many organizations. Insecurity makes people resist change because they see it only as a threat, never as an opportunity. And the way to build self-confidence is to give people a voice, to get them talking, to listen and to trust one another. In his 1995 letter to shareholders, Welch commented: 'Self-confident people don't need to wrap themselves in complexity, "businessese" speech, and all the clutter that passes for sophistication in business, especially big business. Self-confident leaders produce simple plans, speak simply, and propose clear targets.'[16]

We all have expectations from others, stated or unstated; others have similar expectations from us. Being realistic about what to expect and about what others expect can go a long way in keeping our motivation levels high during execution. Think of it this way: The service we provide is similar to providing electricity to homes. When someone plugs in a charger in a socket, it should work. People expect power in their homes to be available round the clock. So, during any outage, there is great distress, which continues till the power resumes. But nobody cares what happened on the other end for power to resume.

How Realistic Are You? Self-assessment

Far from being a single learnable skill, being realistic is actually an amalgam of several elements—think of it as a sort of 'winning combination' of optimism, confidence, motivation, willpower and assertiveness, as well as smartness and self-efficacy. The process is time-consuming, since there is no formula for striking the right balance between all these elements. It is an art that you must develop on your own; and therefore your journey will also be unique. The process requires not only drive and initiative, but tenacity and perseverance to follow through on our efforts till fruition.

We conclude this chapter with an exercise that will help you in this process. The selection in this questionnaire combines the constituent elements of being realistic, while reflecting situations you may have come across in your day-to-day life.

The scores to be used are as follows:

1 = the response stated never applies to you
2 = the response stated rarely applies to you

3 = the response stated sometimes applies to you
4 = the response stated often applies to you
5 = the response stated always applies to you

Scenario #1

Situation	Your Response	Score
Towards the end of a hectic week, your manager informs you that there's a new deliverable that will require you to work right through the weekend. He seems apologetic, but there's no way around this.	While it requires you to cancel all your weekend plans, you agree to your boss' request since you feel this is a genuine situation that has come up at the last minute and no one else is qualified to pick this up.	

Scenario #2

Situation	Your Response	Score
You've arranged a pot-lunch party with close friends and you've tried a new recipe for the occasion. However, no one else seems to like it.	You take the feedback in your stride without getting upset since you know that a new recipe is often not your strength and it only gets better with practice.	

Scenario #3

Situation	Your Response	Score
In the annual day function, you were expecting to be felicitated for a project well executed. However, to your surprise, the award is shared between you and another person from a different team.	You are fine with this realizing that it is more about meeting the company's need than your individual need. You congratulate your co-winner and strike up a conversation with him.	

Scenario #4

Situation	Your Response	Score
In the appraisal discussion, your boss informs you that the promotion you were so looking forward to hasn't come through. He says that you need more time, to make it to the next level.	Even though you're very disappointed at that moment, you schedule another meeting with him later when you are calmer. You give him a patient, attentive hearing to understand what changes are expected from you.	

Scenario #5

Situation	Your Response	Score
You are part of a sales team that makes a pitch for an important potential client. Even though your presentation went well, the contract was ultimately bagged by a competitor firm.	You ask for a debrief from the client to understand what could have been done better. While you know you can't win every time, this process has given you valuable experience which you can leverage in future proposals.	

- If your total score is between **5** and **11**, you need to work on being realistic.
- If your score is between **12** and **18**, it indicates that you are already well on your way to being realistic.
- If your score is between **19** and **25**, then you already have an evolved measure of being realistic.

For many of these questions, you may well have a sense of what the appropriate response should be. But make sure you select the option that most accurately describes your behaviour or response, as opposed to what you feel it should be and save a copy for future reference. Our hope is that when you return to this questionnaire—say, a couple of months later—you'll find that your scores have improved, indicating some progression in the journey to becoming realistic.

8

Being Reflective: Are You Missing the Big Picture?

Being Reflective: Theory and Practice

The *Oxford English Dictionary* defines 'reflection' as 'serious thought or consideration'. It is concerned with consciously looking at and thinking about our experiences, actions, feelings and responses and then interpreting or analysing the same in order to learn from them.[1] Reflection helps us identify things we would otherwise probably not even notice or give any thought to. This quality deepens and enriches our experience of learning about ourselves and others. It holds the key to emotional enablement through the enhancement of both our personal competence and social competence. The problem is that most of us are quick to judge but slow to self-reflect.

Being reflective requires a certain degree of stillness. 'We cannot see our reflection in running water. It is only in still water that we can see'—so goes the Zen saying. However, against the backdrop of such a speed-oriented culture, being mindful, reflective and meditative tend to become synonymous with inactivity and idleness, whereas being seen as a person of action is lauded. Given the hectic, activity-filled lives that we lead in today's world, we develop a bias for action at all times, perhaps even unknown to ourselves.

While action and drive are certainly important for our growth, so is learning, and real learning comes from not just doing, but also reflecting on what we've done, and learning from those reflections.

Think of the practice of reflection as the act of holding a mirror before our actions. This allows us to contemplate them after the fact, but we can also use this metaphorical mirror to project it forward, visualize an important event in the future, imagine how we would conduct ourselves in that situation and thence be able to assess in advance the impact that we will make through our actions.

Reflection

Figure 8.1

Developing a habit of reflection and continuous improvement can't be done overnight, only gradually over time. Of course, along the way we will make mistakes and occasionally revert to our old behavioural patterns, but it's important to understand that only through repeated reflection, course-correction and renewed action will real transformation begin to take root within us. We need to reflect on several fronts: on our self-management—are we being transparent, adaptable and optimistic; on our relationships—are we able to inspire, influence and develop others; and on organizational awareness—are we cognizant of associations and networks, of varied dynamics and the rapidly changing environment? These are some important things we need to keep in mind.

Which sounds doable enough, of course. Yet, in practice, why is this so difficult to master? Part of the answer is that being reflective is a process that entails not just diligent, meaningful introspection but one that requires the inherent acceptance of one's faults and shortcomings, the ability to swallow one's pride and to say—yes, I made a mistake. Keeping one's ego in check is one of the hardest things to do. The failure to reflect and not learn from mistakes means that we maintain status quo, without feeling the need to alter our existing patterns of actions or behaviour, under any circumstances.

Another challenge we all commonly face is the lack of time. We are always so busy *doing*, so where's the time to think deeply about things, especially in hindsight? Also, there may be negative emotions and feelings associated with the memory of an unpleasant event, and the last thing we want to do is revisit or relive it. For instance, think of the last time you had a fight with a loved one. Chances are you felt angry, sad and depressed, but outside of recognizing those feelings, you consciously avoided analysing the situation, to prevent invoking a whole set of negative feelings, whereas the natural human urge would have been to think back on it.

But you probably shut out those feelings by forcing yourself not to think of the incident. Only true reflection on the event, however, can help prevent a repeat of the same unpleasantness or mistakes in the future.

At the workplace, a pressure situation pushes us to take hasty and sometimes rash decisions without adequate reflection. For example, a unilateral decision taken in a team meeting, without hearing out any specific objections or alternative points of view or thinking through the possible repercussions.

There's also a cognitive bias at play, hampering our reflectiveness. This is the tendency to search for, interpret and favour information that confirms one's pre-existing beliefs or hypotheses, while giving less consideration to alternative, novel possibilities. Psychologists also call this the confirmation bias or the myside bias. Thus, we often find that a mother has trouble seeing flaws in her child's behaviour and a lover is blind to a partner's faults. When we interact with someone we dislike, we notice their annoying habits more than their pleasant ones.

When we hear a point of view which is different from ours, we tend not to notice it or give it less importance. In the process, we rob ourselves of an opportunity to step back, reflect and learn. As this behavioural pattern establishes itself over time, we feel inclined to surround ourselves with individuals who hold the same beliefs and opinions as ours, or who we know are unlikely to disagree openly. This aspect has serious implications for leaders, since it precludes almost all chances of constructive criticism or candid self-examination.

To be truly reflective, we need to inculcate proper behaviours and habits so that every day, we become a slightly better version of what we were a day before. Once this trait becomes second nature, we can reflect deeply on all our previous experiences dispassionately and learn from them. But acquiring true reflectiveness is not just a matter of habit and focus; it also involves allowing a degree of humility into our personalities.

That's Not Cricket!

In India's 1981 tour of Australia, a Dennis Lillee in-cutter caught Sunil Gavaskar in front of his stumps and umpire Rex Whitehead raised the finger at what seemed was a fair call. Gavaskar, still rooted to the spot, claimed his bat had made contact with the ball and was most reluctant to leave the field, shaking his head vehemently even as he did so. Clearly, this dismissal was not a decision he agreed with.

But then something happened, possibly abuse hurled from the spectators, so that Gavaskar snapped, stopped mid-track, turned around, walked back to fellow opener Chetan Chauhan and instructed to walk off the pitch with him, in protest. As the spectators booed, the Indian captain continued to march off the field, and only the poised ministrations of the manager of the Indian team ensured that Chetan Chauhan returned to the crease, as the new batsman Dilip Vengsarkar came out to join him.

Fast forward to 2014. Over three decades after the infamous walkout incident in the Melbourne Test cricket which generated huge controversy, former India captain Sunil Gavaskar apologized for his aggressive act of dissent. In his own words: 'I regret the decision. It was a big mistake on my part. As India captain, I was not supposed to act in that manner. In no way, I can justify my act of defiance. Whether I was out or not, I should not have reacted that way.'

So, what prompted this change of position? Even if there was an internal realization, why go public with it? And why did it take him so long to do so? We, the authors, have not had occasion to interview Gavaskar on this matter. Rather, in seeking to answer these questions, we have relied on our understanding of how people's psyches evolve over time, as they gain in maturity.

In the midst of a sudden stressful situation, our better judgements are held in abeyance, the brain reverting to its primeval fight-or-flight response. And in this instance, it is evident that Gavaskar fought, rising to the bait. The degree of affront the cricketer may have felt was closely tied to his ego. Depending on which, his immediate sense may have been that it was not just a personal insult, but an abuse thrown in the face of the entire team, and identifying himself as not just the leader of the Indian cricketing team, but equating himself with it, may also have been instrumental in his decision.

But time had put a distance between him and that event, and as he reflected on it in later years, Gavaskar would have come to realize that notwithstanding the fairness of the umpire's decision, his behaviour on the field that day exemplified neither the spirit of the sport nor his own standing. Perhaps he needed sufficient time, not just to reflect upon his action all those years ago, but also to express his regret publicly and maturely. Reflection involves the internal acknowledgement of one's mistakes, but thereafter, it takes both courage and humility to declare it openly. Which is what Gavaskar did.

True reflection becomes second nature only when a person has developed a habit of critical thinking over time, and also has an open mind. In our assessment, these are the attributes that led Gavaskar to ponder over the Melbourne incident in the cricket Test, regret his behaviour inwardly and eventually admit his mistake, albeit years later. Without an open mind, one can ponder over an action or decision several times over but with the same result—a justification of one's behaviour. With such a mindset, you can't make any real change in your behaviour because you can't change what you don't acknowledge as being flawed.

Soldier or Scout?

One thing that almost all of us are really good at is rationalizing our actions and behaviours. Everyone has their own reasons as to why they behave in a certain way, right down to a petty thief who has justified to himself as to why he needs to steal to make a living. Being reflective presupposes not only the ability to think but also the mindset to make internal changes to shape our emotional makeup into a state of maturity. Only then would we make progress towards higher emotional enablement. Being reflective requires us to have a critical and open mind.

The diagram below presents the interplay between critical thinking and openness of mind.

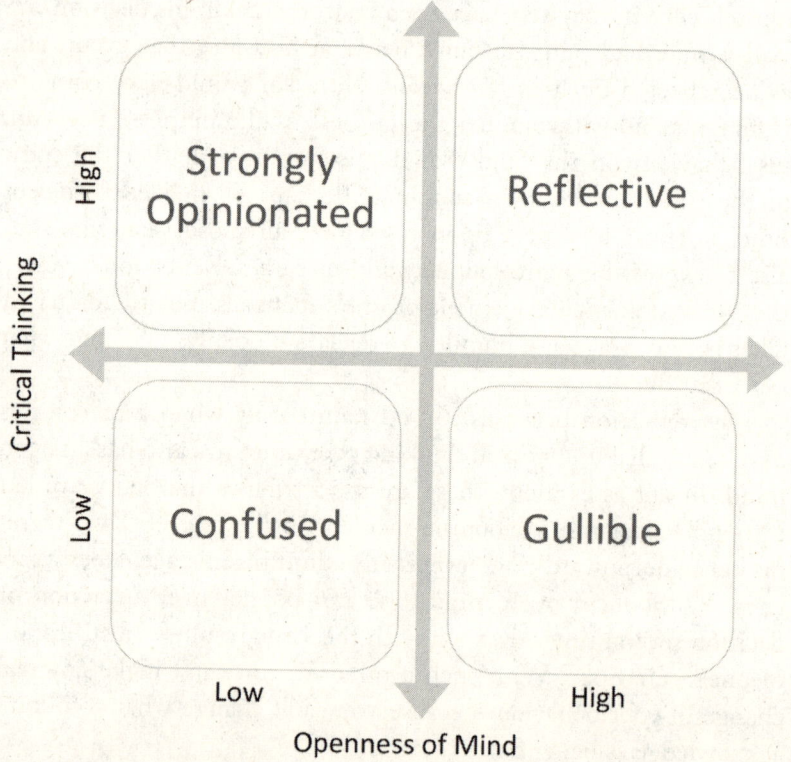

Figure 8.2: Critical thinking vs openness of mind

A person who is open-minded but low on critical thinking is gullible and can be easily influenced by others. On the other hand, if someone is high on critical thinking but not open to others' ideas, he comes across as strongly opinionated and inflexible. At the workplace, probably all of us have come across people who will go to any length to explain with logic as to why their idea or opinion is the right one. The thing is, such people are frequently in error, but rarely in doubt! Ironically, their often-higher IQ which gives them the ability to think critically becomes the very reason for a lower EQ because they are unable to effectively understand and relate with others and change for the better.

To better understand this particular style of thinking, consider the roles of a soldier and a scout during war. A soldier goes to war knowing fully well that the singular goal of his mission is to defeat the enemy. In combat, he needs to either kill or get killed. But along with soldiers, there are also scouts, whose jobs are no less significant. Their task is not to attack or defend but only to gather intelligence and understand ground situations. They are only interested in finding out what's happening and gathering information without bias. That the enemy's troops are moving in a direction, that they have approached a bridge in a certain location across a river, and so on.

The two archetypal behaviours of soldier and scout characterize how we typically process ideas and interact with others in our daily lives.[2] Whenever we approach others with a soldier mindset, it becomes important for us to win the argument. Unknowingly, we make sure each conversation becomes an argument. Our opinion needs to win over that of others, and that's what matters most. We develop a tendency to either attack or defend an idea rather than truly understanding what that idea is and reflecting on its merits and demerits. Scientists call this 'motivated reasoning', where our unconscious motivations, desires and fears shape our thinking and our way of interpreting information. Consequently, interactions tend to become confrontations, and before long, we alienate ourselves, people around us are uncomfortable opening up with their opinions, be that in business meetings or at the dinner table.

We'd be better advised to embrace a scout mindset and develop that over time. The process requires us to overcome our prejudices and biases and be able to see different points of view in a candid, unbiased fashion, even if those are contrary to our beliefs and not necessarily pleasant for us. We need to move away from the notion of 'winning all the time'.

Once we've got here, when we encounter something that contradicts our values or expectations, it makes us intrigued and curious, instead of feeling defensive and insecure. It's only when we take a step back and manage to say, even if inwardly—*Hmm ... I may have been wrong!*—that we pave the way for real behavioural change within ourselves. Having acknowledged a different point of view, we then need to have the conviction and self-confidence to admit our change of stance without lowering our self-worth. As we advance in our personal and professional lives, our need for reflection and openness of mind also grows. Unfortunately, as we grow older (and also scale up the professional ladder), more often than not, we actually close ourselves to new experiences, people and information.

Imagine two equally senior professors at an institute. One of them has a great appetite for new knowledge and ideas. He engages enthusiastically with students and junior faculty even from lesser known universities. Despite his advanced age, he is highly energetic and is seen as a leader in his domain. The other professor, by contrast, has not produced anything new for years now. Although he made many contributions in his earlier years, his stature and pride prevent him from reaching out and collaborating with people who are outside his circle of followers. He has fallen into what is known as the 'expert trap'.[3]

Regrettably, the expert trap is equally prevalent in corporate circles, where it's called 'the CEO disease'. In many management circles, the CEO and senior leaders think of themselves as infallible. Their perpetual self-aggrandizement makes them oblivious to how their actions and behaviours impact the people they lead. Not unsurprisingly, they're surrounded by yes men and others who're afraid to speak their minds candidly. And on the rare occasion when any difference of opinion does arise, the leaders immediately go into the 'soldier mindset' mode.

Consequently, this low level of emotional enablement of leaders creates a dangerous disconnect between them and their teams. But the onus lies on leaders themselves to be cognizant of such traps and ensure they do not fall into them. It is imperative that they remain open-minded, allowing them to continuously learn, adapt and evolve. The personalities of leaders and how team members adapt or react to them introduces an additional dimension (and complication!) about our ability to be reflective, as the account below from Dhiman Banerjee, an advertising executive, shows.

It's Not 'What', but 'Who'—Dhiman's Story

> This was at my previous job. I was based in Delhi; as part of the creative team for a top ad agency, my role as advertising manager for a marquee FMCG client gave me a lot of creative leeway, so I was quite happy with my work. Our firm on the whole promoted an informal working style, which suited me, and I particularly enjoyed the SpeakEasy Huddle, company-speak for our fortnightly meeting where folks from the creative and account teams got to brainstorm together and also network with members of the leadership team. One of these was a tenured advertising account director, a guy I'll call Venu.
>
> 'I've had history with him', as the saying goes—those earlier dealings with him, albeit few, had not gone well and I carried a perception that he was incompetent in his job. This feeling was reinforced on talking to some of his current team members, who described him and his management style as 'nit-picking, micromanaging and eternally serious', and I was glad not to be part of his team. Then one day, my boss called me and told me that the firm was undergoing some reorg [reorganizing]. I'd still have the same portfolio and role at the client's, but some streamlining was being done at the management level and my new boss was going to be Venu!

> The months that followed were pretty rough. My interactions with Venu were neither pleasant nor productive. I hated his detailed instructions, which I didn't feel I needed, or the needling questions on every aspect of a campaign that until that point I'd been managing on my own, not just efficiently but to the great satisfaction of the client. Although I tried to play along for a while, inwardly I could feel myself growing increasingly demotivated. Before long, I found myself another job.

If a number of you can relate to this situation, that's because it is a common one. Studies show a high correlation between an employee's engagement and motivation and his relationship with the boss. The saying 'People join companies and leave managers' is rather true. But reflecting on that time, Dhiman is now struck by a keen insight about himself: While working for Venu, he was not in a position to reflect on his relationship with his boss nor could he objectively consider the feedback he got from him, as they sounded like criticism. Instead, Dhiman had become completely defensive and closed. This is an example of the confirmation bias at work—because Dhiman had an inherent dislike of Venu, whatever the latter said in terms of appraisal or feedback was seen by Dhiman through skewed, coloured lenses.

And this aspect—our personal dislike of people clouding our sense of objectivity—is something we always need to keep in mind, as we set about developing our reflectiveness and taking it to the next level. It's not good enough to be at our best only with certain individuals with whom we get along well. In fact, the need for it is a lot more in relationships (or people) where things aren't going all that well. We need to reflect on whether we are biased towards (or against) any specific co-workers and also on what could be causing that bias. This is even more important for leaders, as they need to constantly reflect on interactions with all team members, irrespective of whether they are his favourites or not.

The same applies to our personal lives. But once we've reached home, we tend to forget to apply those same principles with parents, spouse or children. We take them for granted or believe that with them we can just 'be ourselves', without having to worry about perceptions. And the skills that we work so hard to gain and apply, we often discard them where they could be most useful.[4]

The Art of Candid Feedback

All of us have prejudices, opinions, beliefs and experiences that make us view everything, including ourselves, through a 'lens', so that often we are not able to see things as *they* truly are, but see them as *we* are. This lens comes in the way of understanding ourselves objectively, leading to a big gap between how we see ourselves and how others see us. One good way of bridging this gap is to ask for feedback from others and thereby uncover our blind spots.

Interestingly, while blaming, gossiping or spreading rumours, telling people off and getting unsolicited advice is widespread, giving genuine unbiased and constructive feedback isn't. The intention behind giving feedback is always to help people get better rather than to point fingers, and it stems from care and support for the other person, not from an exertion of power and anger, which feels humiliating and abusive. For feedback to be constructive, it has to be specific and not vague or judgemental. Consider two statements expressing the same observation:

A. In our team meeting yesterday, I noticed your body language was a bit passive.
B. You lack energy in meetings.

Clearly, in this case Statement A is more helpful to the recipient of the message. In Statement A, 'I noticed' brings in a certain distance and, at the same time, objectivity—making it an observation as opposed to being a value judgement about the other person's abilities. Statement B has an accusatory tone and leaves no room for understanding the other person's point of view—here, we have already made up our minds about the other person's shortcomings.

Feedback looks at ways to get better in the future, whereas criticism and blame are about the past. It's not about venting anger or getting something off our chest. The past is important to the extent that lessons can be drawn from it, for the future. Saying 'You may want to leave more time for questions in your subsequent presentations. I noticed people felt that there was no time for discussion' is different from 'Why were you so rigid in your presentation, not allowing any room for discussions?'

Recall the last time you asked someone for genuine feedback, not approval. Not asking 'Did you like my talk?' (the other person being always induced to say yes), rather, 'What is the one thing I could have done better in my presentation?' How often have you hesitated to speak to a colleague, about some aspect of his behaviour or communication which you felt needed improvement, because the other person might not take it well? And when it comes to people close to us (spouse, children, siblings), it only gets tougher because with them, we tend to avoid seeking and giving feedback. The reason is simple—this is the one of the toughest things to do!

Our need for feedback starts only when we build both curiosity and a willingness to learn. Asking for feedback requires humility as well as courage, as we make ourselves vulnerable to criticism. Absorbing the feedback requires self-confidence so that we can take it positively without diminishing our self-worth. We all have a deep need for social acceptance and we want to be accepted and liked; having our imperfections pointed out to us goes against this need.

From a neurological standpoint, adverse feedback can be perceived by the brain as a social threat, triggering the fight-or-flight response. This is why when we give feedback (think of a typical performance appraisal discussion), we often get immediate responses of 'That's not true', 'That's not fair' or 'That's not balanced' or 'You don't understand'. The other person gets defensive. The brain has perceived a threat and has triggered off the fight response. The way to counter it is to recognize that the feeling of being threatened does not automatically mean that we are facing an actual threat.

When asking for feedback, we also need to prepare ourselves to hear the truth. We may not get objective feedback just because we have asked for it. For the person giving the feedback, there may be conflicting values of honesty and harmony. 'Should I be fully honest with my friend? What happens if I ruin the friendship?' he might be thinking. So, we need to go out of our way to get honest feedback. While there's no formula for this, the following steps will go some way in obtaining candid feedback.

It will help to tell the feedback provider that he's helping you by being truthful. It's useful to ask what you can do better going forward rather than what you did wrong in the past. This tends to make people more comfortable while giving feedback. Asking more than once provides the other person multiple opportunities, again increasing the comfort level. Then comes the most difficult part—to be able to receive the feedback without judgement. You need to listen openly and carefully, listening to understand, rather than listening in order to respond. Show your curiosity, ask for examples. You need to curb the urge to defend, resist, explain or push back. The desire to defend becomes a lot stronger when you feel some of the feedback is incorrect. But even if part of it is wrong, you need to focus on the component that is right, just take it all in and thank the other person for being honest with you. You can process all of it a later time and decide for yourself which parts to act on.[5]

Effective feedback is also about timing and permission, ensuring that the receiver is in the right frame of mind to absorb it. Without this, it remains unsolicited advice. For instance, if someone's presentation has just ended badly, the person would not be in a good mood and is less likely to be open to feedback at that time. So, while you are eager to give feedback since you may know what exactly went wrong, you need to resist the urge to do so right away and need to push it to a later time when the person has recovered from the situation. And when you think the time is right, always ask for permission first. 'Do you have a few minutes for some quick feedback?' Or 'There is something I would like to share with you. Would you be interested?' It helps the receiver to be mentally prepared for the feedback, positive or negative. And be respectful of the answer. If the person says that he isn't ready for it or does not have time now, let it be. Chances are he will come around to you later, once he is ready.

Here's another thing to watch out for. We tend to sandwich any negative feedback in between positive messages, in the hope that it would mitigate the impact. So instead of giving it straight, we end up saying 'I really like your presentation but...' Often, this leaves the other person confused and the main message can get lost. Also, the positive message will not carry the right impact and will be seen as just a softener. When we want to say something nice, we can give feedback which is positive and not mixed with the negative. 'Hey, just wanted to tell you that you did an excellent job answering those questions' can be a powerful way of motivating others.

While the 'what' and the 'how' of feedback are powerful, it is the 'who' component that matters even more. We are far more open to receiving feedback from people whom we trust and admire. So, if we want others to take our feedback seriously, the onus lies on us to build rapport and be trustworthy in what we say or do. If we want others to give us honest feedback, they need to trust us implicitly and say what's on their mind without fear of retaliation. And if we want feedback on a continuous basis, we need to act on that feedback. Simply requesting it or even listening carefully without interrupting is of no use if we don't implement some, if not all, of it. People quickly realize that the exercise is done merely for effect and promptly stop giving feedback.

Feedback is intense and powerful communication. A single conversation can make or break a relationship. Hence, we need to be careful both while giving or receiving feedback and keep working on it to master it. Done right, it can transform us or bring real positive change to someone who then goes on to contribute more powerfully. Done poorly, it can make us or the other person feel hurt, humiliated and diminished, who then contributes far less.

Action-Reflection

Whenever we are faced with a setback—a missed promotion, an important client presentation that did not go well, defects in deliverables or products, delays in shipping and transportation leading to heavy penalties—we have a natural tendency to think back on the situation. However, we need to ensure that it is reflection in the true sense of the term, not just aimless brooding degenerating into self-pity, self-hate or negative emotions against persons we hold responsible for the issue. This in turn makes it almost impossible for us to move forward in a positive spirit. What we have to consciously develop are the mindset and practice of going from a problem to a solution.

For self-reflection to be genuinely transformative, we need to make it a part of our daily lives, by allocating some time to it each day, if only just five minutes, thereby consciously moving away from the 'doing' mode every moment that we are awake. Over time, this will become a habit. Once we've reached this stage, we should then focus on devoting additional time, weekly, fortnightly, monthly and so forth, and chalk out a full schedule for reflection.

The table below, culled from the work of Peterson, provides a schedule that you may wish to use.[6] But as with most projects, it's not the planning that is the most difficult part; it's the execution. So, as we start this journey, we have to make sure there are no gaps or missing days in our routine. We really need to do these mini-reviews at the same time every day. If we can set ourselves a conscious trigger (such as 'right after dinner'), this will help establish the habit.

Daily (1 min)	What new thing did I try today? What worked well? What didn't? What one thing will I do differently tomorrow?
Weekly (5 min)	What progress did I make last week? What do I need to focus on next week?
Monthly (10 min)	How am I doing on my development/ learning objectives? What do I need to do to keep growing/ learning?
Quarterly (15 min)	What capabilities should I be developing? Where am I making excuses for something I need to take responsibility for?
Annually (1 hour)	Whom do I want to be? What inspires me and fuels my passion? What values do I want to live by? How am I doing against them? What do I need to do in the next five years to accomplish what matters most?

Figure 8.3: A calendar for reflection

The Big Picture

As we sharpen our skills, be it personal or professional, self-reflection helps us to identify mistakes or areas of improvement. However, sometimes, we get so caught up in thinking of incremental changes that we tend to lose focus on the big picture or the end objective. Asking ourselves continuously 'Am I doing things right?' (e.g., better, faster) diverts our attention from a more fundamental question: 'Am I doing the right things?' The first one is about efficiency, the second about effectiveness. While both are important, the second one raises our level of self-awareness. A highly skilled print media marketing professional can keep honing his current skills but would be foolish to ignore the emerging Digital Age. He will need to learn new skills, sometimes from scratch, which are more relevant for online marketing.

Thinking beyond efficiency has big implications in the workplace. Back in the day when I joined corporate life, I remember one of my managers telling me—'I want to make myself redundant in my current role in a year's time.' I found it a bit confusing at that time; only much later did I fully grasp the power of that sentence. What he was essentially telling me was that he was getting ready for the next level. Focusing totally on his current role would have been an excellent strategy for making himself indispensable. But here he was, trying to do the exact opposite by trying to be redundant! His ability to focus on the big picture helped him achieve a higher level of self-awareness.

Even an accomplished, well-respected leader can benefit from this dual thinking mode. As a leader, he takes tough decisions, provides direction and motivates his people. Those are about efficiency. But growing his team requires the team members to eventually come out of his shadow and become leaders themselves. For that to happen, the leader needs not just decision-making but also delegation skills; he needs to not just provide answers but ask questions; he must not only exert control but also create empowerment. By doing these things, he would greatly enhance his effectiveness as a leader. Having said that, it is also hard to do, which is why even well-known, charismatic, larger-than-life leaders often leave behind a leadership vacuum and a trail of uprooted followers because they have failed to truly create leaders.

Sometimes, being mindful of our emotions can help us turn our attention to the larger question of effectiveness. Emotions are like a signalling system and help us to communicate better with others and understand ourselves better. Consider the example of Shiva who was constantly inundated with work, had high stress and high irritation levels at work. But as he became more aware of his emotions, it occurred to him that what he felt was not just stress, it was also disappointment with some career moves he had made, and fear and anxiety about the future. He then started to question whether he was on the right career path.[7]

To see beyond the current situation and into the future, one requires unconstrained thinking. For Shiva, to start thinking about a career change is essential but also difficult if he feels he is stuck in a rut. For a business struggling to generate money, it is difficult for management to envisage a vision, mission and strategy for the organization. When we reflect, we can ask ourselves several 'what-if' questions to move us beyond efficiency. 'If my current role in my organization gets outsourced, what should I be doing?' Or, 'If I have all the money in the world, what is it that I would want to do with my time?' This technique helps us to see beyond the immediate and the obvious and enhances our self-awareness.

As we see in Peterson's list of questions in Figure 8.3, the nature of questions moves toward effectiveness as the duration gets longer. While reflecting on 'what worked well' or 'what progress did I make last week' on a daily or weekly basis helps us get better in what we do, reflecting on 'what capabilities should I be developing?' (quarterly) makes us connect with the big picture. Only having such a perspective can really address even larger questions such as 'Who do I want to be?' (annual) going forward.

Over and above self-reflection and seeking feedback, getting a personal coach can be an effective way to open ourselves up for more introspection. A powerful technique that coaches apply is the 'as-if shifts' and the as-if questions help build positive visualizations. Let's explore some as-if shifts. Let's say you are stuck in a situation and unsure of the way forward. The coach will ask—'Think of a person who you implicitly trust and respect and is also competent in this area. If that person were in your place, what do you think he would do? What advice would he give you?' This is a point-of-view shift and gets us past our own mental blocks. Another example could be—'What if you actually had the information needed? How would you be responding to the request when the required information is available?' Such an information shift helps us gain clear access to other pieces of information which we may not have thought of. A function shift such as 'If you could change any part of the system, what would that be?' automatically creates a broader perspective. And if the response to that question is 'I am not in a position to change the system', the coach could resort to the magic question—'Suppose you had some magic powers and could alter things to suit yourself, where might you begin to make some changes?' The idea is for the coach to cross the hurdle of self-limiting beliefs to help us see how things might look on the other side. With practice, some of these techniques can also be incorporated in our self-reflection.

For us to fully embrace emotional enablement, it takes time and practice which ultimately causes personal transformation. And being reflective holds the key to personal transformation. It requires a foundation of openness, an ability to face our own shortcomings, be honest with ourselves and endure the pain that comes with realizing that we are not all that we might have thought we were. But once we build that foundation and are willing to change, being reflective through self-reflection, feedback and coaching is a powerful way to building personal and social competence.

Towards a Higher Reflectiveness Index

From the earliest philosophical musings on the subject to findings from neuroscience, our understanding of reflectiveness has come a long way. Over the years, the practice and benefits of being reflective have attracted their share of attention among researchers as well as industry practitioners. There has been concerted focus on its effectiveness, particularly in the education sector (both teachers and students), medicine and healthcare. There is now greater recognition of the benefits of the reflective practice, at the workplace and in our personal lives.

The self-scoring exercise given below can help you get an accurate picture of how reflective you are. The questionnaire draws from existing literature and surveys, presenting situations you may have experienced in your daily life. Mark a tick against the number that most accurately describes your attitude or actions.

The scores are to be allotted as follows:

1 = the response stated never applies to you
2 = the response stated rarely applies to you
3 = the response stated sometimes applies to you
4 = the response stated often applies to you
5 = the response stated always applies to you

Questions	1	2	3	4	5
1. After experiencing an unpleasant situation in the workplace or at home, I think over my actions to see if I could have done anything differently under the circumstances.					
2. In preparing for an important event, such as a key meeting or a client presentation, I anticipate possible questions that might come up.					
3. I analyse important actions taken by my supervisor in the workplace to better understand the reasons behind his decisions.					

4. I consciously keep time aside on a daily, weekly and monthly basis to reflect on experiences and actions.				
5. I actively seek and obtain objective feedback about myself from friends and co-workers.				

- If your total score is anywhere between **5** and **11**, then there is still a fair bit of work to be done before you can call yourself a reflective individual.
- If your score is between **12** and **18**, it indicates that you have an inherent understanding and appreciation of reflectiveness and need a bit more consistency in making it a part of your personality.
- If your score is between **19** and **25**, then you are already at a stage of maturity, with regard to becoming reflective.

Your first attempt may yield a score that is disappointing, perhaps even shocking. If so, you may be sure that many before you have been in this same spot. While there is no fast-track formula for increasing your overall reflectiveness index, perseverance and the diligent habit of a self-review will certainly come in handy, in making you successful.

In this chapter, we have focused on aspects of reflectiveness and why it is important for us to develop this attribute over time—not just as a management stratagem for resolving issues, but as a life skill. Like the other dimensions of EQ, the process of making progress on it is a journey in itself, and as you consider the subject more deeply, you will see that these dimensions are not closed compartments in themselves but relate to and supplement one another.

9

Being Empathetic: Game, Set and Match

As we have seen in our previous discussions, being realistic, reflective and mindful are all essential to building emotional enablement. Empathy is not only vitally important, but takes us further afield in our journey of becoming emotionally mature. While the other three states of being are directed internally, where the focus is on ourselves, being empathetic is essentially about understanding others, gaining social skills and ultimately being able to build deep connections with people. And in that sense, imbibing the first three states of being creates a good platform for becoming empathetic.

What Is Empathy?

Empathy. We hear the term used quite often. But what does it really mean? A Google search on the word throws up over 42 million results, and a YouTube search brings up more than half a million videos. Everyone seems to be talking about it, and yet when you ask around what it really means, we hear a diverse range of answers from different individuals. For many, empathy is almost a synonym for compassion, pity and sympathy. But from an EQ point of view, all these terms are in fact quite distinct from each other.

Think about it for a moment. When we pity someone, in the very fact that the other person is an 'object of pity', there's an inherent sense of superiority that we feel, but we're not putting ourselves in that person's shoes. Sympathy certainly goes a step further. It involves the acknowledging of another individual's hardships and extending a hand to provide comfort and assurance. For instance, a doctor, having discovered a severe illness in a patient, may try to comfort him and his family after breaking the bad news to them. But no more.

Empathy, in comparison, is the ability to identify, understand and *feel* another's situation, concerns and motives. At the workplace as well as in our personal lives, we sometimes get to hear this: 'I can imagine what you're going through.' But often, such utterances may be just lip service or good intentions. Simply mouthing such words doesn't necessarily make them true. And here's the critical difference: a person *expresses* sympathy, but *shares* empathy. Empathy is deeper, in that it helps forge more meaningful connections between individuals or between a leader and his team members.

Empathy indicates a graduation from being self-aware or self-focused to a more sharpened and sensitive awareness of people's emotions. Picture this scene. You are driving to work and at the traffic lights, you're approached by a man selling boxes of tissues. You may ignore the person and just look away without feeling anything at all. Or you may feel bad for the person, looking at his state, seeing him do such a tough job on a hot summer day. This, however, reflects your own distress at the situation, together with your helplessness or inability to change it. You may even buy a box of tissues, but this only helps to assuage your guilt. In many such situations, if you are primarily focused on alleviating your own distress, you may simply avoid uncomfortable situations and not try to understand the other person's mental state.

In contrast, if you focus on this street vendor's thoughts and emotions, you can genuinely feel for him. Not feeling *the same as* him, possibly, but still, feeling *alongside* him. You may want to know what he is feeling by simply asking a question or beginning a conversation with a kind word. You have now successfully moved from sympathy to empathy.

Why Is Empathy Important?

When we are sympathetic, we often try to improve the situation. If someone shared with us something that is very painful, we try to put a silver lining around it. We try to make things better. However, it can have the opposite effect. The fact of the matter is, if someone shares something really difficult with you, he or she would rather you say, 'I don't even know what to say' than 'Don't feel bad', or worse, be judgemental by saying, 'You should not feel that way'. Rarely can a response by itself make the situation better. What makes it better is connection. Let's look at some typical instances.

Scenario A

Statement: 'I had a terrible day and am feeling miserable.'
Sympathetic: 'Very bad, no? Just forget about it. Let's go and eat something.'
Empathetic: 'Would you like to share what happened?'

Scenario B

Statement: 'I think my marriage is falling apart.'
Sympathetic: 'I know you are feeling bad.'
Empathetic: 'Thanks for sharing this with me. Means a lot.'

Scenario C

Statement: 'I have the terrible sense that my son is into drugs.'
Sympathetic: 'Don't worry, it will get OK.'
Empathetic: 'I see. Please let me know if I can be of any help.'

As we can see from the examples above, sympathy by itself is not a bad thing at all. However, empathy fuels true connection, while sympathy, even if felt genuinely, falls short of this. The reason emotions are so powerful is that they move us. Thinking or analysing leads to conclusions whereas emotions lead to action. Take the example of philanthropy. We all know that having money does not necessarily make one more generous. That may sound counter-intuitive but the fact is that people give not so much because they have so much that they can share a bit of their wealth but because they empathize with people who can't make ends meet. And it is for this reason that poor people give out a bigger share of their earnings than richer people since they are able to imagine and empathize with the suffering of other poor people.

Genuine empathy requires us to both think and feel what the other person could be going through. The first part, when we try to think like the other person, is Cognitive Empathy, sometimes also referred to as 'perspective-taking'. It is important to recognize the other person's perspective as their truth, even if we do not agree with this perspective. This aspect is of importance to all supervisors, managers and leaders across the board and, in fact, anyone who works with teams. Understanding the thoughts of others helps in calibrating one's responses, where there is disagreement or conflict, and proves critical in cool-headed decision-making in managing stressful situations at the workplace. At the same time, it does not mean that leaders with empathy tend to agree with everyone's views or try to please everybody. Instead, they consciously consider employees' feelings to arrive at key decisions.

When we feel physically with someone else's feeling, as though these emotions were somehow contagious, that is known as Affective Empathy. A person with affective empathy will not only recognize that his friend is feeling sad (cognitive empathy) but will also feel sad along with his friend. This allows us to genuinely tune in to the other person's inner world of feelings and emotions. Others' emotions and what they're going through give rise to perfectly mirrored emotions and feelings, triggered through our own nervous system. Neurologically speaking, this emotional contagion is explained by means of the mirror neuron system, which we shall discuss in detail later in the chapter.

Emotional contagion has huge implications in the world of business. We often come across managers who complain that their teams have all the resources, tools and database, but appear to lack energy. What they fail to realize is that the team's energy is a direct reflection of the manager's energy, thanks to emotional contagion. When a leader is calm, happy and energized, those qualities get reflected in the way his organization or team behaves and performs. You may have observed in your workplace—a leader walks into a meeting looking down and tense, and even before he says a word, his body language itself is enough to suck the life out of the room.

Such is the power of emotional contagion. Leaders, by the very dint of their position, exert a disproportionate impact on the moods and feelings of their team members. Studies have shown that emotional contagion play a significant role in work-group dynamics; people do not live on emotional islands and team members vicariously experience moods at work, wherein these moods ripple out to affect not only other team members' emotions but also to influence their group dynamics and individual cognitions as well as attitudes and behaviours. Thus, everyone's, but especially the leaders', emotions and behaviours can lead to tangible ripple effects in their teams and organizations.[1]

It is important to keep negative emotions in check, as they are highly toxic and spread fast. Keeping them in check means not trying to cover them up but being able to balance them out with realism and optimism. The leader needs to *live* this ethos on a daily basis. Authenticity becomes key here, since faking positivity or an empathetic attitude can't be sustained for long. It may be possible to say you're thinking and feeling one way when you're actually thinking and feeling another, but it's likely that your true feelings will give you away, as your vocal, facial, tonal and postural cues will not be in alignment.

In recent years, several studies have been conducted, which link empathy to business results. One of them recorded a positive correlation between emotion recognition ability and annual income. The finding was that the better people are at recognizing emotions, the better equipped they are to navigate their way through the politics of their organizations and interpersonal aspects at work.[2]

Positive correlations have also been found between empathy on the one hand and increased sales and performance in a diverse workforce on the other. Empathy helps us understand how or why others are reacting to situations, and this sharpens our people skills. Some of these studies are available on the website of The Consortium for Research on Emotional Intelligence in Organizations.[3]

Empathy is important for several dimensions of engagement such as collaboration, problem-solving, conflict resolution, and human functioning in general. Social scientists describe it as a 'social glue, binding people together and creating harmonious relationships'. Empathy leads to today's much-needed qualities of compassion and caring. The ability to see things from others' perspectives itself breaks down biases and stereotypes and paves the way for tolerance and acceptance of differences across cultures and geographies, an aspect of vital importance in a globalized world.

Are You Being 'Hawkish'?

No, we're not asking if you are in the habit of bulldozing over everyone else during team meetings, making sure yours is the only opinion still standing! Rather, we want to know whether you are watching yourself like a hawk, insightful and sharply dispassionate. Imagine a hawk in the sky, rising a hundred feet above the ground, yet with its unerring eye on every little detail down below—a rock, the trees, or some creature sliding under a blade of grass. If you could watch yourself like that, every little reaction, every word that comes out of you, especially in moments of great stress or crisis, wouldn't your behaviour and actions be different from what they otherwise are?

And while you're doing this mind exercise, think through any such instances in the recent past, and reflect on your behaviour in those situations. What would be some of the things you'd have observed about yourself? The aspirations or hopes being dashed, the anger and frustration, the helplessness in not being able to connect with someone close to you, the pain of being misunderstood, or perhaps the not-quite-so effective habit of hiding your insecurities under the veneer of self-confident glib talk? Note them down.

Being 'hawkish', in this sense of the term, allows you to arrive at a more objective understanding of your own behaviour. The best position to be in is to be able to take notice of your emotions, and how they reveal themselves through your behaviour, in the heat of the moment, real-time, as the situation unfolds. If you're able to do this, you will find that you've discovered the ability to slow yourself down and take in all that is in front of you. This way, your brain is able to register all the information or stimulus that it receives and then process it, before you act.[4]

Getting to this stage requires practice and time, and as with the other states of being that we have discussed in this book, it's a journey. But if you can think through some typical situations, play them out in your mind as a sort of script, observe yourself and the other person(s) from a more detached point of view, and think of ways in which you could change some of your own responses; that's a good place to start.

Here's one such example.

You're a leader in charge of a large team involved in operations and HR. Deadlines are stringent, work pressure is perpetually high and the top management relentless—everything was needed *yesterday*. One particularly busy morning, on wrapping up an important team meeting, you're sitting silently by yourself, inside your office. A key team member taking care of HR, and whose inputs were critical in reaching a decision, was conspicuously absent from the meeting. The operations piece cannot function in isolation, and you can't take a unilateral decision on what is essentially an HR matter. So, there will now have to be individual briefings and another unscheduled last-minute meeting, and all this will take up more time—time you don't have to begin with.

She was absent without notice or any reason! Now you're waiting for her to turn up, offer some feeble excuse or simply shrug and clam up when you give her a piece of your mind. Does she not get the importance of these daily meetings? Is this callous attitude on her part not an undermining of your authority, of your position? Isn't this just another way of showing disrespect? You can't afford to have in-person chats with every team member who doesn't bother to attend, to update them on the key discussion points—surely she understands that much!

Your blood begins to boil. And the more you brood on this, the angrier you get. So that when she does come in, a mumbled apology on her lips, you pay no attention to what she might have to say. In a steely voice, you ask her to come in, shut the door behind her, and then, you just let loose. After a verbal lashing from you, she gets up and leaves quietly, headed straight to the cafeteria, bursting to tell her friends about this monster of a boss that she has to put up with. As the day progresses, the unfinished business from the morning still needs to get done, you're in a foul mood and there's bad blood between the two of you.

But now, try to see if you can change this screenplay.

A. Being Mindful. Take your mind to the point where the team has dispersed after the meeting. Become the 'hawk' and observe yourself from this vantage point. You know very well that this calm before the storm is only serving to raise your temper. Admit to yourself inwardly that you are getting very angry. And that with this mood, things will get unpleasant. This acceptance is almost half the battle won. Once you realize this, you will see there are far more fruitful ways of utilizing your time. So instead of letting your anger fester, you can busy yourself preparing for another meeting that's coming up, catch up on any backlog emails, make calls, or ping your friend to confirm that he's still on for that working lunch. Or simply get up from your seat, take a walk around the floor, go into the pantry and fetch yourself a glass of water. Greet colleagues you pass by, be aware of the sights and sounds around you.

B. Being Realistic. Your angry outburst may intimidate your team member and will almost certainly alienate her, but will it send the right message? You may satisfy your ego with this behaviour, but will it get the work done? Is this going to put her in a frame of mind where she can focus on the work at hand? After all, you still do need her inputs to arrive at that important decision and make your report! So maybe when she comes in, you could tell her that you're upset and explain why, underscoring the criticality of the meeting that she has missed, instead of demonstrating through ill-chosen, hurtful words just how upset you are.

C. Being Reflective. By now, you've attended to other work and not allowed that unfruitful morning meeting to prey on your mind. You've cooled down and are ready to do some dispassionate, clear-headed thinking. You realize that this absence on the part of your team member is a one-time thing, not an ongoing pattern. Maybe there's some reason for this, apart from sheer spite for you as you may suspect, that's getting her late in the mornings? Something as common and genuine as a flat tyre? And perhaps she did call you while on the road but couldn't get through due to a bad network connection? Or maybe she's had an emergency at home that couldn't wait? Think through this for a bit, and you will realize that you've made assumptions about her absence that may not be true. So how about asking her for an explanation and preparing yourself to hear her out, instead of making unfounded assumptions on your own?

D. Being Empathetic. If you've followed steps A to C diligently, your temper hasn't shot through the roof. On the surface, nothing has changed; the facts are still the same; yet you've taken your mind, thoughts, attitude and behaviour through a process. You're more accepting, rather than exacting, and instead of a rant that could only go in one direction, you're more open and ready for a dialogue. So when she comes in, don't interrupt her, let her go through with what she has to say. In fact, go a step further and listen carefully, without judgement or bias; don't allow your angry emotions to creep back in. Tell yourself that you're no longer angry. There's always a bagful of ready tricks that can make the other person feel guilty or small;

don't resort to them. Instead, make an effort to put her at ease, ask if she wants a cup of coffee and have her seated comfortably in your office. Engage in the conversation, nod to indicate that you've understood her point of view and conclude the meeting objectively with a plan for getting the work done. The meeting over, now compare the results of this interaction with what would otherwise have taken place.

Children, Mimicry and Mirror Neurons

They say children are born actors. And in a sense, that's true. A lot of learning in the young, formative years is through observing others and imitating. Words and language, expression and body language—are largely acquired through this process. Children take note of and then mirror the behaviour patterns of adults around them. Likewise, emotions, and in particular empathy, are said to work in much the same way, through mimicry and mirroring those of others.

This revolutionary idea comes from the work of researchers such as Dr V.S. Ramachandran, a noted neuroscientist and author of bestselling books, including *The Tell-Tale Brain: A Neuroscientist's Quest for What Makes Us Human*.[5] In his research, much of the emphasis is on mirror neurons. As the name suggests, these neurons, located within the cortex of the human brain, are triggered when a person observes an action or emotion in another. The neurons then mirror the behaviour of that other person, as if that action was being performed (or emotion being felt) by the observer himself.

Ramachandran's belief is that mirror neurons are about as integral to our understanding of psychology as DNA has been to biology. He claims that advances in our understanding of the functioning and role of mirror neurons will explain a wide range of human mental capacities such as empathy, imitation learning, and the evolution of language, phenomena such as artistic creativity and even conditions such as autism. He asserts that mirror neurons can not only help simulate other people's behaviour but also can be turned 'inward', to create second-order representations of one's own earlier brain processes. This could be the neural basis of introspection, and of the reciprocity of self-awareness and other awareness.

And he is not alone in making these assertions. Marco Lacoboni, Stephanie Preston, Frans de Waal, Jean Decety, Vittorio Gallese and a host of other researchers also believe that the mirror neuron system has a key role to play in human empathy. Several experiments using measures such as fMRI and EEG have shown that certain sections of the brain become active when people experience an emotion, such as sadness, happiness or amusement, when they see another person experiencing the same emotion.

According to some studies, the activation of mirror neurons (Ramachandran also calls them 'Gandhi Neurons') results in the release of empathy hormones such as prolactin, which then act on the brain and body to produce a mirror emotion, reaction or condition. Ramachandran has another hypothesis, which states that mirror neurons may provide a concrete neurological explanation for self-awareness, a key human attribute long held to be intangible and philosophical.

The study of mirror neurons, which began in the early '90s, is still fairly new and many of the theories of its chief proponents are yet to be conclusively proven. However, regardless of whether mirror neurons by themselves are the answer to all these diverse aspects, there is now increasing agreement among researchers that human beings are naturally equipped with the apparatus for observing, processing and reciprocating emotions. And evidence of it can be seen even in everyday situations.

You walk into a room to see some people seated around a table, laughing loudly. The little bits of words they put in are drowned out in that laughter. They notice you, smile and invite you to take a seat, still grinning broadly. And if you were to be astutely aware of your own expressions, you'd feel a smile spreading on your own lips. So what has just taken place? Your mirror neurons are reflecting the feelings of the people present and you start feeling as they do—even though you've just joined them and haven't been involved in their conversation.

The fact of the matter is that as human beings, we are all connected to each other emotionally, and we are wired to feel its contagion. This realization is of great import, not just in our personal relations with colleagues, friends and loved ones, but also in the shaping of our behaviours at the workplace and key business strategies. For example, we can channelize this natural power of empathy to put ourselves in the minds of our customers, discern their desires and tastes, understand the pressures of our suppliers, the needs of our employees as well as the mindset of our competitors. Therefore, even in the selfish, cut-throat competition of the business world, empathy can be a very powerful weapon.

So What's Not Working?

And yet, empathy isn't by a long chalk the first thing you encounter in the workplace. Quite the opposite, in fact—many managers are characterized by their team members as being hassled, impatient and unsympathetic. This doesn't mean that managers are uncaring slave drivers. But unlike the technical, industry and domain knowledge that they gained over the years through focused training and application, they haven't necessarily been trained for leadership, to resolve interpersonal conflicts, to handle or manage the aspirations, ambitions and frustrations of team members.

In effect, a manager is expected to be not just a boss, but a trusted mentor and friend, to focus not merely on deadlines and product launches, but be invested emotionally in his team. And that's the emotional part of work. However empathetic you want him to be, your manager still has to deliver on the timelines, on the level of quality required of him, to write out reports, make his numbers for the year, make his own bosses comfortable with team progress, then go back home and manage that other part of his life. And that is a tall order.[6]

Which is why many managers, having risen through the ranks, really struggle at this point in their careers, become negative and defensive. Because inwardly, the lack of self-worth they feel is often reflected as distant behaviour, a closed attitude to listening to the suggestions and opinions of his team members. Any change from status quo is perceived as a threat and any suggestion as a criticism, to the extent that sometimes, managing the boss becomes a daunting project for the team members.[7]

A variant of this, particularly in the higher echelons, is the executive isolated in his corner office. This proverbial 'loneliness at the top' is sometimes the product of the executive's own doing, but equally, it is possible (and is often the case) that his immediate circle of juniors and advisors work to this end. This way, they filter out unpleasant information before it reaches him. His main source of connect to ground realities thus cut off, the executive is hampered in his decision-making ability. And if the executive happens to be insecure or temperamental in the first place, the effect is magnified—he is surrounded by a team of sycophants busy putting up mirage-like walls all around him.[8]

How to Increase Empathy

It may seem from this above discussion that we are basically wired for empathy; and yet, our daily stress and strains, hectic lifestyles, and the constant pressure to balance work and life, are all conspiring to make us less so. But it doesn't have to be such a doomsday scenario. The starting point, as we mentioned earlier, is conscious awareness—of ourselves and that of others around us.

Being empathetic requires that we do the following things—listen better, observe and ask questions. And it all begins with having a genuine interest in the other person. If we're genuinely interested, we listen better and are not in a hurry to put forth our views but instead stay focused on the other person.

Dale Carnegie, in the book that has now become a classic—*How to Win Friends and Influence People*—makes an interesting case on this point. According to him, 'you can make more friends in two months by becoming genuinely interested in other people than you can in two years by trying to get other people interested in you.'[9]

And this is no less true when it comes to our relationships at the workplace.

People who put in a lot of effort trying to network and impress and get other people interested in them, their products and companies that they represent may fare worse than those who make it their business to understand their clients. Take, for instance, a salesperson, whose job is to make potential customers interested in his products by creating the right amount of 'noise' and pushing through his products over those of his competitors. But as any successful salesman knows, being genuinely interested in people is a key trait for the job.

To understand what the other person is going through emotionally, we need to be able to read non-verbal cues, not just focus on the words. The fact is that human beings communicate a lot more non-verbally than they do using words. Non-verbal cues include body movements and gestures, gait and postures, tone, pitch, inflexion, even the way one dresses. But what give us huge insight into others are facial expressions.

It has been found that facial expressions are universal; in other words, they cut across race, culture and age. There are seven basic human emotions that have clear facial signals—anger, sadness, fear, surprise, disgust, contempt and happiness—and people throughout the world use them to convey emotions.[10]

Sometimes, when we want to conceal what we are feeling, we try to cover up our expressions quickly. This is often true in organizational settings where people need to be cognizant of the subtle dynamics at work, and so may not want to reveal their real emotions in an open setting. But this covering up still leaves traces, called 'micro-expressions'—expressions that go on and off in a person's face in a fraction of a second. So, a leader needs to be good at reading not just expressions but also micro-expressions.

In the American crime drama TV series *Lie to Me*, Dr Cal Lightman (played by Tim Roth) and his colleagues assist in investigations by interpreting microexpressions and body language. And in the process, Lightman's characters often demonstrate different facial signals and pointers on how to read the expressions. For instance, eyebrows get raised both in surprise and fear but in the case of fear, they get pulled together as well. And when the eyebrows are down and together, it can signal anger. Consider the images below.

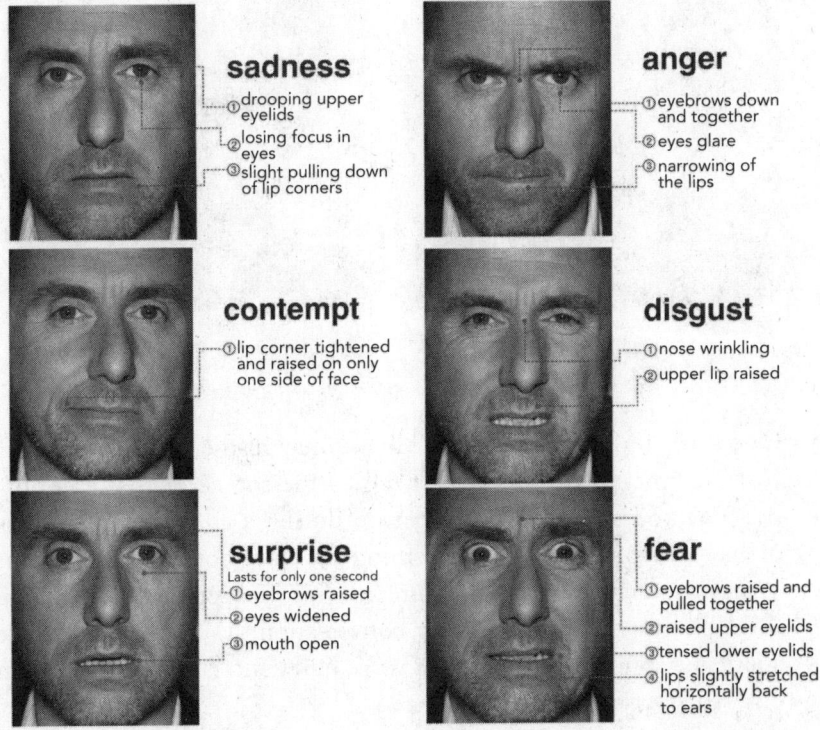

Figure 9.1: Microexpressions

The one expression that's not in the picture above is that of happiness. Most of us feel that it's relatively easy reading happiness in any person's face, sometimes even in his voice—because the person 'smiles'. But then, is the person smiling because he's genuinely happy or out of politeness? It's a subtle difference and most people miss it.[11] A genuine smile activates two sets of muscles—one which helps pulling the lip corners up at an angle into a smile and the other which circles around the eyes and helps pull up the skin below the eye and raises the cheeks (see diagram below). The next time you see a smile, try to notice if the eyes are smiling as well.

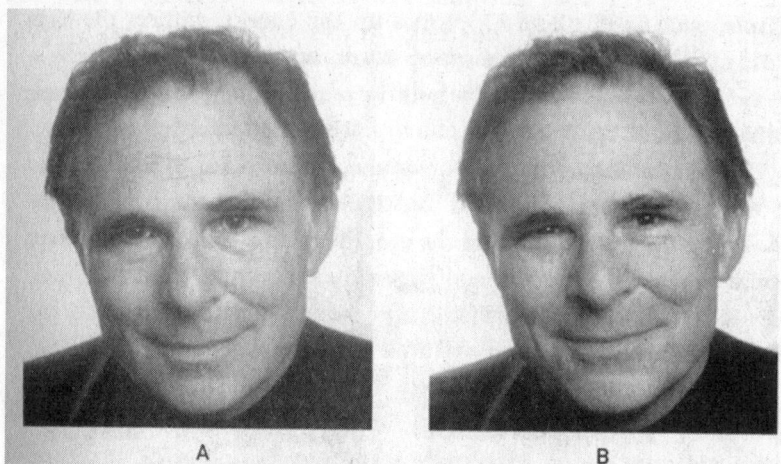

Figure 9.2: Fake vs real smile

One thing to keep in mind: While we may read emotions in others correctly, the expression doesn't tell us the source of that emotion. Suppose you spot anger in a person during a conversation. Is this directed at you? If so, is it something you have done or said, now or earlier? Or maybe the anger is directed onto oneself or towards some third person mentioned in the conversation? We may learn more about the source of the anger if we're quiet and curious rather than obsessing about giving a response.

The Need to Listen

From a very young age, we're taught how to speak, how to read and how to write. However, it is assumed that we will automatically pick up how to listen without any accompanying training. Consequently, most of us grow up to be poor listeners. Indeed, keeping quiet and listening is easier said than done. But why is it so hard? A simple answer is that it's about control. We talk first to own the moment, to take charge and in the process, we prove ourselves by preaching what we know and what we think. Subconsciously, we send a message that we are better, saying—I should speak while you listen. It's our way of setting the rules—this is what we're going to do, and this is how we're going to do it.[12]

Whereas, if I let you talk first, I have no idea what you're going to say. So, I am giving up control of the situation and that's a bit scary. Like stepping into the unknown. However, by giving up control, we end up gaining an upper hand. Right off the bat, we gain trust, which is key to building relationships. We may gain information that helps in solving a problem. As we gain insights, we start to see other people as individuals, not merely as stereotypes. And when the other side feels heard, they are more open to listening. If they feel that you do not 'get' them, they'll be less inclined to listen to you. Most importantly, listening helps in resolving conflict because both parties feel connected and it breaks the 'us versus them' mindset. It creates psychological safety, where both parties feel safe discussing issues openly. The paradox of listening is that by temporarily giving up power—the power of speaking and asserting—we end up becoming more powerful.

In the command-and-control approach to management, communication was directive and top-down. But as the layers get broken down, competition increases and more millennials join the workforce, the style of communication needs to turn more conversational. This has huge implications for today's leaders. Studies show that today's smart leaders engage with their employees more through ordinary person-to-person conversation, rather than giving out commands. This means leaders need to listen more, since ordinary conversations are two-way communication, as opposed to commanding which is unidirectional.[13] The onus lies on the leader to minimize distances—both emotional and physical—between him and his employees. To do that, they first and foremost need to listen to their employees—listen with earnestness and curiosity, which signals both humility and respect for people. That in turn earns them the trust of those who report to them.

How to Improve Our Listening?

One simple way to find out if you are a good listener is to think of your talking/listening ratio in any conversation. If in a ten-minute conversation, you spend seven minutes talking, you're not being a good listener and you're simply dominating the conversation. But you are not alone. Research shows that on average, people spend 60 per cent of conversations speaking about themselves, and this number shoots up to 80 per cent when communicating on social media platforms such as Twitter or Facebook.[14] A good conversation, on the other hand, is like a game of catch. It's impossible to play catch with someone and throw more than we catch. So too, we need to talk half the time and listen in the other half.[15]

And while we increase our listening, we also need to be aware of the quality of our listening. This assumes greater importance when we engage in difficult conversations, say at work. When someone is speaking, notice if you're already thinking about your rebuttal. Are you starting your response with a 'yes', followed by a 'but'? Or, even worse, have you already interrupted the other person? All of these reduce empathy and connection and diminish our chances of building relationships.

We can think of the listening experience as three stages—preparing to listen, active listening and empathetic listening. For good preparation, we need to remove all distractions so that we can focus on the other person and convey that they have our full attention. That means muting the cell phone and putting other work aside instead of trying to multitask. If we are busy with a deadline, it's best to schedule a better time to speak. That way, the other person feels that the conversation is important to you. If the person wants to speak about a sensitive topic, it helps to assure him that he can count on you to maintain confidentiality so that psychological safety is ensured.

Next—active listening. In this stage, we try to understand the full message, including the person's body language and tone instead of just limiting our attention to the words. This helps us uncover hidden non-verbal messages. The other big component of active listening is not to be distracted by our own thoughts and not interrupt people (often the former causes the latter). We need to focus completely on the other person and acknowledge that we are listening by an occasional nod or 'OK'. Also—and this is tough—it is important to avoid any judgement or criticism till we have fully heard out the other person. When we keep debating or play devil's advocate, it reduces the psychological safety and discourages the other side from opening up.

The highest level of listening is empathetic listening. Here, we need to put ourselves in the other person's shoes and try to see things from their perspective. We can summarize what they said in our own words, or use paraphrasing to show them that we understand their perspective. This helps in reducing differences. Last, but not the least, we need to get comfortable with silence. Instead of fearing silence, we need to use it effectively to give people time to finish their message and allow them to reflect on what they have just communicated.

How to Communicate with Empathy?

While listening is critical to building empathy, how we respond and the words we use play an equally important role in building and maintaining relationships. We need to remain curious and ask open questions which can help others articulate themselves fully and open up about their feelings, instead of using closed or leading questions that 'put words in people's mouths'. When we use open-ended questions such as—'Tell me more about that', 'I can understand why you are so upset about this', 'Was this the first time this happened?', 'I would be frustrated too', 'What happened next?' and so on—these mirror the speaker's feelings and make him feel heard and understood. Needless to say, it's not just about uttering the words; we need to be sincere in saying them.

The human connect happens best when the two sides are level, i.e., when each person sees the other as someone like him, as someone he can relate to. Sometimes, without realizing it, we say things that are judgemental and try to one-up the other person. But it is better to refrain from saying things such as 'It's not that bad', 'Don't get so upset over this' or 'It's all going to be fine'. Using clichés doesn't inspire people, so avoid saying things like 'When the going gets tough, the tough get going', or 'The grass is greener on the other side'. Being judgemental also increases emotional distance, so resist the urge to say things like 'Well, if you had programme-managed better...' What works well for a connection is when we open up and share our innermost thoughts and feelings. Sure, that does make us vulnerable, but that is also what makes us human and real.

The need for us to communicate with empathy is even greater when we need to deal with a situation that calls for a courageous conversation. In such situations, the chances of conflict are high and being able to navigate through it using empathy greatly reduces the chance of the other person feeling offended and talks breaking down. One very effective way to achieve this is to talk about our own experiences, instead of 'unloading' on the other, blaming and judging. In the process, we turn the 'you' vs 'me' dialogue to one of 'us' and can stay respectful of the other person even while delivering a hard message.

Let's say one of your team members (let's call him Ravi) is not delivering as per plan. You think something is keeping him from focusing on his work. You decide to have a face-to-face chat with him. In that meeting, a common way to address the issue is by telling him: 'You are not meeting your deliverables on time. You seem to be distracted.' By using the direct address 'you' a couple of times, chances are Ravi is already in a defensive mode by then. Anything more we add, such as 'The other team members are suffering because of this' or 'You need to get back on track fast or else...' only makes matters worse and takes away from the emotional connect. Instead, if you focus on what you observe and feel and believe, you will be able to communicate with empathy and also get the message across. What you could say and its impact is summarized in the table below:

Experience	What you say	How
I observe...	I observe that you have not met the deliverables on time	Share what you observed without interpretation, judgement or evaluation
I feel/felt...	I feel let-down	Share what you feel – be specific and talk about the effect it has on you, not others; talk emotions rather than thoughts
Because I believe/ value...	I feel let-down because I believe we can only be successful if we get full engagement from everyone in the team	Identify what is underneath the feeling – what you need or value; why it matters to you
What I need/ like to do...	What I would really like is to find a way we can work more effectively together	It is a solution-focused conversation; describe what the desired outcome looks like and emphasize benefits; finally, remain open to new outcomes

Figure 9.3: Communicating with empathy

Empathy in Organizations

Today, customer preferences change rapidly, resulting in shorter product life cycles and raising customer expectations, and the need for innovation is felt more than ever before. To stand out, companies need to create emotionally engaging products and services. And the way to do this is to empathize with customers. Moving beyond an understanding of customers to empathizing with them is at the heart of what is known as 'Design Thinking', a notion of design as a 'way of thinking'. Instead of focusing on traditional methods such as past customer data and market research, the process is based on deep research involving real people in their natural environments.

And how can one gain genuine empathy in this approach? By knowing potential customers on a personal and even intimate level, spending enough time with them to see what *they* see and experience what *they* experience. This level of 'customer immersion' generates meaningful 'insights' into human behaviour and it is these insights that hold the key to innovation.

As companies start seeing the benefits of empathy, more and more will embrace the concept. There are now terms such as 'empathy marketing', 'empathy selling' and 'user empathy', referring to user interface. Companies are training customer service folks on empathy. Statements like '100 per cent guarantee' don't cut it anymore. Instead, when dealing with an unsatisfied customer, service agents need to show empathy by choosing words that show that they understand and care, and at the same time acknowledge how the customer feels, instead of defending themselves. Empathy becomes vital during organizational transformation; leaders need to understand their employees' concerns, their barriers to change and reasons behind their resistance. Only then can they achieve true buy-in to make any transformation successful.

The Empathy Index

Researchers, particularly in the domain of psychology and medicine, have been studying the parameters of empathy for several decades now. And in this process, our knowledge of this key human dimension has gained considerably, instruments of evaluation have been refined and made statistically robust, and the underlying scales and mechanisms of measurement have become more sophisticated. One of the earlier measures to enjoy widespread use was the Empathy Scale devised by Hogan in 1969. It contains four separate dimensions of measurement—social self-confidence, even-temperedness, sensitivity and non-conformity; this method was widely in use for a long time.

By the 1980s, with enhanced and more precise knowledge of the constituents of empathy, the Empathy Scale was seen more as a measure of cognitive empathy, one that did not consider any evaluation of the affective component. The Interpersonal Reactivity Index (IRI) was then developed by Mark Davis. The IRI included elements of Perspective Taking and Fantasy, in addition to Empathic Concern and Personal Distress, thereby increasing the capability of measuring different aspects of empathy.

Besides the IRI, two other scientifically validated scales have since been created by researchers to measure empathy—the Toronto Empathy Questionnaire, developed by Nathan Spreng and his colleagues, and the Emotion-specific Empathy Questionnaire, developed by Sally Olderbak and her colleagues. These take into account both cognitive and affective components, and have been developed to a state of maturity, through numerous studies.

However, if there's one single Empathy Assessment that you'd like to take, our recommendation is the questionnaire developed by Berkeley University. This one incorporates elements from the Toronto Empathy Questionnaire,[16] the Interpersonal Reactivity Index and the Emotion-specific Empathy Questionnaire mentioned above, and presents them collated in a simple, online form. The questions, drawing on situations from everyday life, evaluate you on affective as well as cognitive empathy. It also examines the relationship of empathy to aspects such as gender, political, racial and cultural background.

Perhaps the best benefit from this test is the detailed report it generates. Along with a total consolidated score, it gives a break-up for affective and cognitive empathy, an interpretation of the score and suggestions on how to work on your areas of development.

The URL for the questionnaire is given below:
http://greatergood.berkeley.edu/quizzes/take_quiz/14

Against All Odds

We find ourselves at an interesting point in human history. Some would call it a point of inflexion. Globalization has shrunk the world and simultaneously made human contact and communication more complex than ever before. Advances in science have made us reach for the stars and yet, poverty, injustice, oppression and ecological disasters abound in different parts of the globe. Traditions are fading fast to be replaced by new, often unpredictable behavioural patterns in human beings. The workplace that the millennials find themselves in is fundamentally different from the one the earlier generation joined at the beginning of their careers. And this change is incessant.

According to many analysts, over the next twenty years, more than half the world's jobs will have been outsourced—not to India and China, but to automated processes, gadgets, and robots, the standard-bearers of a new omnipotent intelligent technology that will govern the workings of businesses globally. Already, we are beginning to see signs of this in India; employees in large organizations are being made redundant by technology and automation, which are more effective, reliable and economical than human beings.

What would that mean for the future generations? Mass unemployment? How would businesses function with so little human input, where fortunes of giant corporates and their shareholders are guided by competing algorithms that have all been worked out automatically, without human intervention? What would leadership mean in this new and utterly changed world? And how would the institutes of the day educate their children and youth to prepare them for it? The reliance on STEM, which over the last few decades of the twentieth century, helped to fuel growth and productivity, can no longer be the answer, by itself. In fact, nothing we have seen in our times can be extrapolated to give us the solution.

And so it seems that in such an age of ubiquitous automation and robots, times of such ambiguity, philosophy, the discipline that has suffered much neglect in the Digital Age, may yet make a comeback. Philosophy will not be able to conjure masses of new jobs out of thin air. But the practice and study of it can certainly help us rationalize our fears and anxieties, overcome personal biases and enhance our openness to divergent views. It also serves as a constant personal reminder to each of us, to hold fast to our individual values, humanity and empathy.

As if in anticipation of such an era, at least a few countries around the world have started to take the matter seriously. In 2016, Ireland introduced a new optional course for twelve- to sixteen-year-olds, inviting schoolchildren to reflect on questions that for ages have been absent from school curricula. The teaching of philosophy, according to Ireland's president, Michael D. Higgins, is one of the most powerful tools we have at our disposal to empower children into acting as free and responsible subjects in an ever more complex, interconnected and uncertain world, and offers a viable path to a humanistic and vibrant democratic culture.[17]

We conclude with a story taken directly from history books. This tale underscores how, even in the worst of circumstances, it is still possible for genuine human empathy to shine through. Compared to which, our minor bickering at the workplace, the daily battles with deadlines and the tendency to give in to stress, pressure and anger, against our better judgement, are perhaps not so terrible after all.

December 1914. Five months into a new, unfamiliarly terrible war, soldiers on both sides dug themselves into their trenches for a bitter winter. And as the carnage continued through the month, two things became quite evident. First—that after this war, things in the world would never quite be the same again. And second—it was very far from over. And yet, starting on Christmas Eve, at several points along the Western Front, the unthinkable happened. Allied soldiers heard brass bands joining the Germans in their joyous singing. Decorative lights dotted the whole line of their front.

As the morning fog cleared the next day, a few German soldiers emerged from their trenches and approached the Allied lines across No Man's Land, calling out 'Merry Christmas' in English. At first, the Allies suspected it might be a trick. Moments passed, no shots were fired, and the Germans were still walking into the line of fire, unarmed. Wearily, a few British climbed out of their trenches, beyond the barbed wire and into No Man's Land, face-to-face with enemy soldiers.

That tenuous, hand-on-the-holster moment. And then, all that tension melting into the shaking of hands. The soldiers turned around to their own sides, the others cheered from the trenches, waved and scampered out onto the sodden frost-white ground, past barbed wire and shell holes. And in the middle, they all began to all shake hands and swap cigarettes, chocolate and cognac, and stayed out there the whole day. There was even talk of arranging a football match.

Short-lived and unrepeated though it was, through the rest of the devastating war, this Christmas truce continues to be a testament of how ordinary soldiers rose above the roar of guns to reveal their innate humanity and empathy for fellow human beings.

Index

Being Empathetic, 106, 110, 177, 185
   Active Constructive Responding (ACR), 41
   Empathy Assessment, 199
   Empathy Index, 2, 198
   Global Empathy Index, 2
Being Mindful, 4, 106–07, 112, 184
   Mindfulness-based Stress Reduction (MBSR), 127
   Waterfall Metaphor, 119, 123
Being Realistic, 4, 106–07, 109, 136
   Three-box Solution, 137–38
   Progress Principle, 140–43
Being Reflective, 106, 109, 157, 185
   Action/Reflection, 170
   Expert Trap, 164
   Reflectiveness Index, 174
Bias
   Confirmation Bias, 159, 166
   Cognitive Bias, 78, 159
   Illusory Superiority, 108, 138
   Overconfidence Bias, 108, 138, 147

CEO Disease, 164
Competence – Conscious, 96
   Unconscious, 102

Critical Thinking, 162–63

Design Thinking, 71, 197
Digital Age, 54, 73, 114, 172, 200
Disruption, 151

Emotions
   Emotional Brain, 119–22
   Emotional Contagion, 180–81
   emotional enablement (EE), 3–4, 7–9, 28, 47–8, 92, 117, 162
   Emotional Intelligence, 5, 7, 24, 30–31, 35
   Emotional Quotient (EQ), 102
ESTEEM, 4, 7, 93, 100–02, 106
Evolving Organization, 6, 52

Feedback, 32, 44, 46, 58, 67, 86–89, 105, 154, 166–69, 170, 173, 174, 176

Gallup survey, 144
Globalization, ii, 7, 37, 63, 67, 105, 199

Hawkish Behaviour, 182–83

Impulse Control, 39, 60

Index

Industrial Revolution, 48
Innovation, xiv, 66, 70–73, 100, 197
Intelligence Quotient (IQ), 1, 31, 38, 102–103, 145, 163

Knowing-Doing Gap, 124

Meditation, 7, 122–29, 132–33
Micro-expression, 190
Millennials, 1, 5, 6, 7, 38, 74–79, 80–89, 90–92, 193, 199
Mindset, 6, 37, 50, 51, 58, 66, 71–72, 91, 101, 161–65, 171, 188, 193
Monkey Mind, 120
Multitasking, 11, 115, 130
Muscle Memory, 69

Neuroscience
  Amygdala, 121–22, 127, 131
  Amygdala Hijack, 121–22, 131
  Autopilot, 107, 116-17, 135
  Cortisol, 121, 127, 130
  Dopamine, 140
  Functional MRI (fMRI), 126–27, 187
  Electroencephalogram (EEG)/ Alpha, Beta, Gamma, Theta, 128, 187
  Gandhi Neurons, 187
  Fight or Flight, 120, 122, 127–28, 130, 168
  Hippocampus, 128
  Keystone Habits, see also Habit Formation, 141
  Mirror Neurons, 111, 186–87
  Neocortex, 121
  Neurons, 11, 116–17, 186–87
  Neuroscience, 4, 31, 102, 127, 140, 174

Pre-frontal Cortex (PFC), 127
Reptilian Brain, 120
Vagus Nerve, 131
Numbness, 113–14

Organizations
  Aditya Birla, 64
  Adobe, 5, 81
  Apple, 53, 133, 146–47
  British Petroleum, 54
  Facebook, 82, 89, 91, 114, 194
  Flipkart, 55
  GE, 152
  Google/ Googlegeist, 66, 67, 133, 145, 177
  HCL, 84
  Housing.com, 38
  Infosys, 142
  INSEAD, 88
  Mercedes Benz, 71
  Merrill Lynch, 83
  Microsoft, 1, 62
  Mindtree, 61, 133
  Morgan Stanley, 83
  NASA, 144
  NASSCOM, 91
  PricewaterhouseCoopers (PwC), 76, 84
  PepsiCo, 145
  Satyam, 59, 60
  Shell, 54

People
  Bagchi, Subroto, 61
  Birla, Kumar Mangalam, 64
  Cappelli, Peter, 78
  Carnegie, Dale, 189
  Chandrasekhar, R., 91
  Coleman, Mark, 133
  Dacher, Keltner, 57

Dalberg-Acton, Lord John, 59
Duckworth, Angela, 140
Gates, Bill, 62
Gavaskar, 160–61
Goleman, Daniel, 4, 31, 103
Govindarajan, Vijay, 150
Jobs, Steve, 49, 125, 147
Kabat-Zinn, Jon, 123, 127, 133
Kaplan, John, 66
Kennedy, John F., 144, 146
Krishnamurti, J., 126
Lally, Phillippa, 141
Lesser, Marc, 133
Loehr, Jim, 56
Mandela, Nelson, 118, 151
Mihaly Csíkszentmihályi, 148
Mitterrand, Francois, 118
Molinsky, Andy, 68
Moritz, Bob, 84
Nayar, Vineet, 84
Nooyi, Indra, 145
Raju, Ramalinga, 59–60
Ramachandran, V.S., 186–87
Nadella, Satya, 1
Schwartz, Tony, 56
Seligman, Martin, 149

Taylor, George W., 78
Welch, Jack, 152–53
Yadav, Rahul, 38–39
Zuckerberg, Mark, 89
Personal Competence, 103
Pit stops, 129, 131
Post-traumatic Stress Disorder (PTSD), 127
Power Paradox, 56

Relationship Management, 104, 106

Self-awareness, 104
Self-management, 104
Self-reflection, 172
Signature Strengths, 147, 149
SMART Goals, 145–46
Social Competence, 103–04, 157, 174
Soldier or Scout, 162
South Korea, 67
STEAM, STEMMA, 101–02
STEM, 101
Sympathy, 177–78

References

Chapter 2

1. Daniel Goleman, *Working with Emotional Intelligence*, Bantam, 1998
2. Muriel Maignan Wilkins, '7 Signs You Lack Emotional Intelligence', *Harvard Business Review*, 19 May 2015
3. Daniel Goleman, 'How to Be Emotionally Intelligent', the *New York Times*, 7 April 2015
4. Laura Entis, 'At Work, Emotional Intelligence Pays', *Entrepreneur*, 15 December 2014
5. Carl Richards, 'Being Mindful Can Help Guide a Decision', the *New York Times*, 17 October 2014
6. Gable, S.L., H.T. Reis, E.A. Impett, E.R. Asher, 'What Do You Do When Things Go Right? The Intrapersonal and Interpersonal Benefits of Sharing Positive Events', *Journal of Personality and Social Psychology*, 2004, pp. 87, 228–245

Chapter 3

1. O'Toole, James and Warren Bennis, 'What's Needed Next – A Culture of Candor', *Harvard Business Review*, June 2009
2. Walter McFarland, 'Managers in the Digital Age Need to Stay Human', *Harvard Business Review*, June 2015

3. Loehr, Jim and Tony Schwartz, *The Power of Full Engagement*, The Free Press, 2003
4. Jonah Lehrer, 'The Power Trip', the *Wall Street Journal*, 14 August 2010
5. Lou Solomon, 'Becoming Powerful Makes You Less Empathetic', *Harvard Business Review*, April 2015
6. Tomas Chamorro-Premuzic, 'Why So Many Incompetent Men Become Leaders', *Harvard Business Review*, August 2013
7. 'The Psychology of Power', the *Economist*, 21 January 2010
8. Kingshuk Nag, *The Double Life of Ramalinga Raju: The Story of India's Biggest Corporate Fraud*, Collins Business, 2009
9. Ray Williams, 'Why We Need Kind and Compassionate Leaders', Psychology Today, August 28, 2012
10. Prasad Kaipa and Navi Radjou, *From Smart to Wise: Acting and Leading with Wisdom*, Random House India, 2013
11. John Traphagan, 'Why "Company Culture" Is a Misleading Term', *Harvard Business Review*, April 2015
12. McKinsey & Company, *Reimagining India: Unlocking the Potential of Asia's Next Superpower*, Simon & Schuster Inc., 2013
13. McKinsey & Company, 'Learning from Google's Digital Culture', *McKinsey Quarterly*, June 2015
14. 'Loosening Their Ties: Corporate Culture in South Korea', the *Economist*, 28 November 2015
15. Tsedal Neeley, 'Global Teams That Work', *Harvard Business Review*, October 2015
16. Andy Molinsky, 'Emotional Intelligence Doesn't Translate Across Borders', *Harvard Business Review*, April 2015
17. Erin Meyer, 'Navigating the Cultural Minefield', *Harvard Business Review*, May 2014
18. Sarah Cliffe, 'Companies Don't Go Global, People Do: An Interview with Andy Molinsky', *Harvard Business Review*, October 2015
19. Rigby, Darrell K., Kara Gruver and James Allen, 'Innovation in Turbulent Times', *Harvard Business Review*, June 2009

20. Gary Hamel, 'Innovation Starts with the Heart, Not the Head', *Harvard Business Review*, June 2015
21. Tom Kelley and David Kelley, 'Reclaim Your Creative Confidence', *Harvard Business Review*, December 2012
22. Jon Kolko, 'Design Thinking Comes of Age', *Harvard Business Review*, September 2015
23. Warren Berger, 'The Four Phases of Design Thinking', *Harvard Business Review*, July 2010

Chapter 4

1. 'Millennials at Work: Reshaping the Workplace', PwC survey, 2011
2. Edmund Clarence Stedman (edited by), *A Victorian Anthology, 1837–1895*, Cambridge: Riverside Press, 1895
3. Amy Gallo, '4 Things You Thought Were True About Managing Millennials', *Harvard Business Review*, July 2014
4. Bruce N. Pfau, 'What Do Millennials Really Want at Work? The Same Things the Rest of Us Do', *Harvard Business Review*, April 2016
5. Howe, Neil and William Strauss, 'The Next 20 Years – How Customer and Workforce Attitudes Will Evolve', *Harvard Business Review*, July-August 2007
6. Grant McCracken, 'Boomers, Stop Yelling at Gen Y to Get Off Your Lawn', *Harvard Business Review*, October 2012
7. Nick Shore, 'Millennials Are Playing with You', *Harvard Business Review*, December 2011
8. Kristin Naragon, 'Email Is the Best Way to Reach Millennials', *Harvard Business Review*, November 2015
9. Dorie Clark, 'Stop Wasting Your Time on Work Calls', *Harvard Business Review*, March 2016
10. Glaser, Judith E. and Ashley Blundetto, 'Reassess Millennials' Social Sharing Habits', *Harvard Business Review*, March 2015
11. Dhar, Vilas and Jia Fetherson, 'Impact Investing Needs Millennials', *Harvard Business Review*, October 2014

See Also – Walter Frick, 'Millennials Are Cynical Do-Gooders', *Harvard Business Review*, May 2014

12. Andrew Winston, '10 Sustainable Business Stories that Shaped 2015', *Harvard Business Review*, December 2015
13. Andrew Winston, 'What VW Didn't Understand about Trust', *Harvard Business Review*, September 2015
14. Andrew Winston, 'Keeping Up with the Clean Label Movement', *Harvard Business Review*, October 2015
15. Bob Moritz, 'The U.S. Chairman of PwC on Keeping Millennials Engaged', *Harvard Business Review*, November 2014
16. Vineet Nayar, 'Handing the Keys to Gen Y', *Harvard Business Review*, May 2013

    See Also – Vineet Nayar, 'Letting Gen Y Lead a Management Makeover', *Harvard Business Review*, February 2011
17. Gino, Francesca and Bradley Staats, 'Developing Employees Who Think for Themselves', *Harvard Business Review*, June 2015
18. Cal Newport, 'Solving Gen Y's Passion Problem', *Harvard Business Review*, September 2012
19. Eric Hellweg, 'Gen X and Gen Y Respond to Workplace Divides', *Harvard Business Review*, July 2007
20. Tamara J. Erickson, 'Gen Y in the Workforce: HBR Case Study', *Harvard Business Review*, February 2009
21. Erica Williams, 'Debunking the Millennials' Work Ethic "Problem"', *Harvard Business Review*, April 2010
22. Nanette Fondas, 'Millennials Say They Will Relocate for Work-Life Flexibility', *Harvard Business Review*, May 2015
23. Andrew McAfee, 'Gen Y's Most Perilous Trait?', *Harvard Business Review*, September 2010
24. Meister, Jeanne C. and Karie Willyerd, 'Mentoring Millennials', *Harvard Business Review*, May 2010
25. Karie Willyerd, 'Millennials Want to Be Coached at Work', *Harvard Business Review*, February 2015
26. Henrik Bresman, 'What Millennials Want from Work, Charted across the World', *Harvard Business Review*, February 2015

27. Lori Goler, 'What Facebook Knows about Engaging Millennial Employees', *Harvard Business Review*, December 2015
28. Lou Solomon, 'The Top Complaints from Employees about Their Leaders', *Harvard Business Review*, June 2015
29. Andrew McAfee, 'Millennials Won't Change Work; Work Will Change Millennials', *Harvard Business Review*, July 2010
30. Tom Davenport, 'Can Millennials Really Change the Workplace?', *Harvard Business Review*, December 2008
31. 'HR Goes the Whole Mile to Keep Millennials Happy', the *Economic Times*, 21 July 2015
32. Andrew O'Connell, 'Millennials Are Entering a Changed Workplace. Not', *Harvard Business Review*, November 2014
33. Charan, Ram, Dominic Barton and Dennis Carey, 'People Before Strategy: A New Role for the CHRO', *Harvard Business Review*, July-August 2015
    See Also: Rock, David and Beth Jones, 'Why More and More Companies Are Ditching Performance Ratings', *Harvard Business Review*, September 2015

Chapter 5

1. Robert N. Charette, 'What Ever Happened to STEM Job Security?' *IEEE Spectrum*, 5 September 2013
2. Michael S. Teitelbaum, 'The Myth of the Science and Engineering Shortage', the *Atlantic*, 19 March 2014
3. 'India Facing Shortage of Engineers in S&T: DRDO DG', the *Hindu*, 29 January 2013
4. Vince Bertram, 'STEM or STEAM? We're Missing the Point', the *Huffington Post*, 26 May 2014
5. Johan Roos, 'Build STEM Skills, but Don't Neglect the Humanities', *Harvard Business Review*, 24 June 2015
6. Daniel Goleman, *Emotional Intelligence: Why It Can Matter More Than IQ*, Bantam Books, 1995
7. Daniel Goleman, *Working with Emotional Intelligence*, Bloomsbury, 1998

8. Daniel Goleman, 'Primal Leadership: The Hidden Driver of Great Performance', *Harvard Business Review*, 2001

Chapter 6

1. Hougaard, Rasmus and Jacqueline Carter, 'How to Practice Mindfulness Throughout Your Work Day', *Harvard Business Review*, March 2016
2. Maria Gonzalez, 'Your Car Commute Is a Chance to Practice Mindfulness', *Harvard Business Review*, November 2013
3. Thich Nhat Hanh, *Happiness*, Parallax Press, 2009
4. Jon Kabat-Zinn, *Wherever You Go, There You Are*, Hyperior, 2205 (10th edition)
5. Arnie Kozak, *Wild Chickens & Petty Tyrants: 108 Metaphors for Mindfulness*, Wisdom Publications, 2009
6. Susan David, *Emotional Agility – Get Unstuck, Embrace Change, and Thrive in Work and Life*, Penguin Random House, 2016
7. T.W. Rhys Davids, *Dialogues of the Buddha, Part II*, Oxford, Great Britain: Pali Text Society, (1959) [1910], pp. 322–346
8. Kabat-Zinn, *Wherever You Go, There You Are*, Hyperior, 2205 (10th edition)
9. Hermann Hesse, *The Glass Bead Game*, Vintage/ Random House, 2000
10. J.Krishnamurti, *Meditations*, selections made by Evelyne Blau, Shambala, 2002
11. 'How Does Meditation Change the Brain?' *Scientific American* Video on YouTube
12. Williams, Mark and Danny Penman, *Mindfulness – An Eight-Week Plan for Finding Peace in a Frantic World*, Rodale, 2012
13. Kabat-Zinn, *Wherever You Go, There You Are*, Hyperior, 2205 (10th edition)
14. 'The Mindful Revolution', *Time*, 3 February 2014
    See Also – Virginia Heffernan, 'The Muddied Meaning of Mindfulness', the *New York Times*, 14 April 2015

15. Bohlmeijer, E., P.M. ten Klooster, M. Fledderus, M. Veehof and R.A. Baer, 'Psychometric Properties of the Five Facet Mindfulness Questionnaire in Depressed Adults and Development of a Short Form', *Assessment*, 2011, 18: 308–320
See Also – Baer, Ruth A., Gregory T. Smith, Emily Lykins, Daniel Button, Jennifer Krietemeyer, Shannon Sauer, Erin Walsh, Danielle Duggan and J. Mark G. Williams, 'Construct Validity of the Five Facet Mindfulness Questionnaire in Meditating and Nonmeditating Samples', *Assessment*, 2008; pp. 15, 329, originally published online 29 February 2008
– Baer, R.A., G.T. Smith, J. Hopkins, J. Krietemeyer and L. Toney, 'Using self-report assessment methods to explore facets of mindfulness', *Assessment*, 13, pp. 27–45.

Chapter 7

1. Eyal Winter, 'Feeling Smart – Why Our Emotions Are More Rational Than We Think', Public Affairs™, 2014
2. Todd Zenger, 'The Case Against Pay Transparency', *Harvard Business Review*, 30 September 2016
3. Teresa, Amabile and Steven Kramer, *The Progress Principle – Using Small Wins to Ignite Joy, Engagement and Creativity at Work*, Harvard Business Review Press, 2011
4. Charles Duhigg, *The Power of Habit*, Random House, 2012
5. Ibid.
6. *European Journal of Social Psychology*, Eur. J. Soc. Psychol., 2010, pp. 40, 998–1009; published online 16 July 2009 in Wiley Online Library (wileyonlinelibrary.com) DOI: 10.1002/ejsp.674
7. 'Infosys 2020 Goals: $20b Revenue, $80,000 Revenue Per employee', *Business Standard*, 18 June 2016
8. Gallup Global Workplace Report, 2014
9. Bob Allen, (edited by), 'NASA Langley Research Center's Contributions to the Apollo Program', Langley Research Center, NASA; Retrieved 1 August 2013

10. PepsiCo website: http://www.pepsico.com/Purpose/performance-with-purpose/our-goalshttp://www.pepsico.com/Purpose/performance-with-purpose/our-goals
11. Walter Isaacson, *Steve Jobs*, Simon & Schuster, 2011, p. 379
12. Mihaly Csikszentmihalyi, *Flow – The Psychology of Optimal Experience*, HarperCollins e-books
13. Buckingham, Marcus and Donald Clifton, *Now, Discover Your Strengths*, Gallup Organization, Free Press, 2001
14. Linley, P. Alex, Stephen Joseph, Martin E.P. Seligman, *Positive Psychology in Practice*, John Wiley & Sons Inc., 2004
15. Vijay Govindarajan, *The Three-box Solution*. Harvard Business Review Press, 2016
16. Robert Slater, *29 Leadership Secrets from Jack Welch*, McGraw Hill, 2003, p. 68

Chapter 8

1. Atkins, S. and K. Murphy, 'Reflective practice', *Nursing Standard*, Vol. 8, No. 39, June 1994, pp. 49–54
2. Julia Galef, 'Why You Think You're Right – Even If You're Wrong' (Ted Talk)
3. Monique Valcour, '4 Ways to Become a Better Leader', *Harvard Business Review*, 31 December 2015
4. Ed Batista, 'How to Not Fight with Your Spouse When You Get Home from Work', *Harvard Business Review*, 12 April 2016
5. Susan David, 'How to Manage Your Emotions without Fighting Them', *Harvard Business Review*, 28 Nov 2016
6. David B. Peterson, PhD, 'Advanced Coaching: Accelerating the Journey from Good to Great' – Presentation made to Congresso Brasileiro de Coaching, San Paulo, Brasil, 14 Nov 2013

Chapter 9

1. Sigal G. Barsade, 'The Ripple Effect: Emotional Contagion and Its Influence on Group Behavior', Yale University, *Administrative Science Quarterly*, December 2002

2. Momm, Tassilo, Gerhanrd Blickle, Yongmei Liu, Andreas Wihler, Markeike Kholin and Jochen I. Menges, 'It pays to have an eye for emotions: Emotion recognition ability indirectly predicts annual income' (Research paper), *Journal of Organizational Behavior*, 2014
3. http://www.eiconsortium.org/
4. Bradberrry, Travis and Jean Greaves, *Emotional Intelligence 2.0*, TalentSmart, 2009
5. V.S. Ramachandran, *The Tell-tale Brain: A Neuroscientist's Quest for What Makes Us Human*, W.W. Norton & Company, 2011
6. Thomas Teale, 'The Human Side of Management', *Harvard Business Review*, November-December 1996
7. Gabarro, John J. and John P. Kotter, 'Managing Your Boss', *Harvard Business Review*, 2000
   See also – Fast, Nathaniel, Ethan Burris and Carolien A. Bartel, 'Insecure Managers Don't Want Your Suggestions', *Harvard Business Review*, 24 November 2014
8. Ron Ashkenas, 'How to Overcome Executive Isolation', *Harvard Business Review*, 2 February 2017
9. Dale Carnegie, *How to Win Friends and Influence People*, Random House UK, 2004
10. Paul Ekman, Ph.D, *Emotions Revealed: Recognizing Faces and Feelings*, Holt Paperbacks, 2004
11. Frank, M. G., P. Ekman and W.V. Friesen, 'Behavioral Markers and Recognizability of the Smile of Enjoyment', *Journal of Personality and Social Psychology*, 1993, 64: 83–93
12. Frank, M.G. and P. Ekman, 'Not All Smiles Are Created Equal: The Differentiation between Enjoyment and Non-enjoyment Smiles', *Humor*, 1993, 6: 9–26
    See also – Amy Cuddy, *Presence – Bringing Your Boldest Self to Your Biggest Challenges*, Orion, 2016
13. Groysberg, Boris and Michael Slind, 'Leadership Is a Conversation', *Harvard Business Review*, June 2012
14. 'The Neuroscience of Everybody's Favorite Topic', *Scientific American*

15. 'How a Great Conversation Is Like a Game of Catch', Celeste Headlee, ideas.ted.com
16. Spreng, R.N., M.C. McKinnon, R.A. Mar and B. Levine, 'The Toronto Empathy Questionnaire', *Journal of Personality Assessment*, 2009, pp. 91(1), 62–71

    See also – M.H. Davis, 'A Multidimensional Approach to Individual Differences in Empathy', *JSAS Catalog of Selected Documents in Psychology*, 1980, pp. 10, 85

    See also – Olderbak, S., C. Sassenrath, J. Keller and O. Wilhelm, 'An Emotion-Differentiated Perspective on Empathy with the Emotion-Specific Empathy Questionnaire', *Frontiers in Psychology*, 2014, pp. 5, 1–14
17. Charlotte Blease, 'Philosophy Can Teach Children What Google Can't', the *Guardian*, 9 January 2017

Acknowledgements

In India, we are witnessing an inflexion point where, suddenly, the old command-and-control style of management is completely out of place. However, enterprises are yet to adopt an empathetic, employee-centric stance. When we proposed the idea of writing a book on this topic to HarperCollins India, it immediately resonated with them. Many thanks to Shantanu Ray Chaudhuri for believing in the need for this book, commissioning it and championing it through the course of its making. Without him, *From Command to Empathy* wouldn't have come into being.

Our heartfelt thanks to Debasri Rakshit and Shreya Punj, our editors, for their collaborative approach in shaping the book—working with them has been terrific and we hope they feel the same! We're also indebted to Meera K. for her highly astute final edit of the manuscript, tightening the narrative and bringing the book's key takeaways into sharper relief. Special thanks to Ananth Padmanabhan, CEO, HarperCollins Publishers India, for taking a personal interest in our book and for supporting the underlying ethos—the increasing need for EQ in the workplace.

We are very thankful to Deb Deep Sengupta, president and MD of SAP India, for writing a foreword for the book. We are also grateful to all the eminent figures from industry and academia who have taken time out of their hectic schedules and endorsed the book—Anoop Nambiar, Ashu Garg, Avelo Roy, Deepak Rathi, Dhimant Parekh, Gerald Gaillard, G.D. Gautama, Harish Hande, Hitesh Oberoi, Manish Sabharwal, Prasad Kaipa, Raj Manchanda, Santanu Das, Sourav Mukherji, S.V. Nathan, Sachin Lulla, Shradha Sharma, Tanmay Bandopadhyay, Vikram Kalloo and Vishal Bhola.

During the two years it has taken us to research, draft and redraft this book, both of us have had reduced quality time to spend with family and friends. At times when our zeal has faltered, they've provided the support and succour needed to bring this book to fruition. Our deepest gratitude to Barun Chanda, Manjushree Chanda, Shikha Kakkar (Avik's family) and Tarun Ghose, Ila (Majumder) Ghose, Rati Ghose (Suman's family).

This book is dedicated to them.

About the Authors

AVIK CHANDA (1972–2023) held a graduation degree in economics from Presidency College, Kolkata, and a master's from the Delhi School of Economics. He had over two decades of experience as a management consultant working with Fortune 500 companies, as part of his tenure at PricewaterhouseCoopers and Deloitte. With a successful track record of key organizational and leadership roles, Avik was an independent consultant, advisor and author. His debut novel *Anchor* was published by HarperCollins India in 2015.

SUMAN GHOSE holds an engineering degree from the Indian Institute of Technology–Kharagpur, and an MBA from the Indian Institute of Management–Bangalore. He has over two decades of corporate work experience, having worked in some of the world's top multinational companies such as Cadbury's, Intel, Philips and PricewaterhouseCoopers. Suman is also the co-founder of Inroads Leadership Development (www.inroads.co.in), which equips organizations to achieve great performance and meaningful growth by building critical leadership skills.

HarperCollins *Publishers* India

At HarperCollins India, we believe in telling the best stories and finding the widest readership for our books in every format possible. We started publishing in 1992; a great deal has changed since then, but what has remained constant is the passion with which our authors write their books, the love with which readers receive them, and the sheer joy and excitement that we as publishers feel in being a part of the publishing process.

Over the years, we've had the pleasure of publishing some of the finest writing from the subcontinent and around the world, including several award-winning titles and some of the biggest bestsellers in India's publishing history. But nothing has meant more to us than the fact that millions of people have read the books we published, and that somewhere, a book of ours might have made a difference.

As we look to the future, we go back to that one word—a word which has been a driving force for us all these years.

Read.